PARENTING
SOMEONE ELSE'S CHILD

Ann E. Stressman

Special contribution by
Ruby K. Payne, Ph.D.

PARENTING
SOMEONE ELSE'S CHILD

The Foster Parents'
'How To' Manual

Stressman, Ann E.
Special contribution by Ruby K. Payne, Ph.D.
    Parenting Someone Else's Child: 241 pp.
    Bibliography: pp. 239-241
    ISBN 1-929229-25-9

1. Education   2. Sociology   3. Title

Copy editing by Dan Shenk.

Dedication

This book is dedicated to foster and adoptive parents everywhere. There are certain challenges in keeping a child for a long time and others in keeping one for a short time. An emergency shelter home takes in children without prior notice, until they can be assessed and a longer-term placement can be made. These foster parents may take hundreds of children in their lifetime. Others may take one child, raise that child as their own, and send him/her out into the world with survival skills that have a lasting effect on his/her life and generations to follow.

We need every one of these foster and adoptive homes to fill the needs of every child who comes into the system. No one of us is more valuable than another. So here's to you, foster and adoptive parents. You're special!

I also want to dedicate this book to Dr. Craig Matheson and Dr. Gailord Weeks, both of Fremont, Michigan. They are the most important people in my support system and in the actual day-to-day life of every person in this family and every person who entered my home since 1990. These two men played vital roles in helping my fostering and adopting be successful — and they continue to be strong allies in my retirement. Indeed, I still depend on them as I parent my adopted children and my granddaughter. There would have been no book without them! They also helped me believe that my experience and knowledge could be useful to other parents.

So thank you, Dr. Weeks and Dr. Matheson, for encouraging and supporting the growth and development of this book, just as you nurtured the growth and development of my children.

Table of Contents

A Word from the Author

Throughout history, people have raised the children of others. Some of these children are well-known from the pages of history or the Bible. "Moses was the first foster child," reads a button I sometimes pin to my blouse. But I doubt he was the first.

Today, in some segments of American society, it's common for a child to live with his grandmother, aunt, or even a surrogate parent, with no legal paperwork involved. Grandparents are increasingly given custody of children. The children may have parents who are drug addicted, alcoholic, or homeless, and cannot parent them. One of the parents may be deceased. Teenagers give birth to babies while still in high school, and it has become acceptable in today's society to keep your baby, raising it with the help of your own parents.

But, as with the job of parenting our own children, there has been no class to teach us, no instruction book supplied, no "how to" manual. Foster and adoptive parents are required to attend classes prior to becoming licensed, but caseworkers are so overloaded they aren't always available to give ongoing help and support, even during a crisis. All of this gave rise to this book.

For 20 years I was a foster parent. For the past eight of those years, I have been married to a man who pledged to support me in this endeavor. I also have taught parenting skills to parents of delinquents who become involved in the court system. In addition, I have read widely on the subject of foster and adopted children. Much of my research has been on attention deficit disorder (ADD) and attention deficit hyperactivity disorder (ADHD). I have used ideas from many authors, developed some of them into workable systems for foster children and other "special needs" children, and taken them into the classroom. I have given seminars to parents of these children, as well as attended countless classes myself to gain the latest ADD research data and management techniques. Also, from a general standpoint, I have been a parent trainer, which has involved doing workshops for pre-licensing requirements, as well as conducting ongoing classes for foster/adoptive parents. Much of child management is common sense, and a number of these techniques have been used and adapted by many parents and educators. In preparation for the seminars I've led, I've read hundreds of pages of advice from others, then passed on the cream of the crop to frustrated and struggling parents.

My book is a summary of these ideas, along with my own hard-won insights, in the hope that you can glean some kernel of understanding, some technique, some method to help you and your child succeed. Teachers can't hope to be able to read about every special need. Parents may not have the time or knowledge to sift through the hundreds of new titles hitting the market, all claiming to have "the answer."

It is my hope that I can teach while learning, help while being helped, and make some friends along the way. I believe that if we all help each other, we'll do a much better job of raising the next generation — and save ourselves from having nervous breakdowns in the process!

As you grow and learn, so does your child. As your family benefits, so does the community. If there is a healthy relationship between you and your child, both lives will be richer and happier in the long run. Send me a letter and let me know how you're doing ... Better yet, look me up when you're in the neighborhood. The house may be a mess, and I might not be able to find the coffee, but we'll laugh and cry together — and hug our children all the while.

-"Mama Ann"

On Children

By Kahlil Gibran

And a woman who held a babe against her bosom said, Speak
to us of Children.
　　And he said:
　　Your children are not your children.
　　They are the sons and daughters of Life's longing for itself.
　　They come through you but not from you,
　　And though they are with you yet they belong not to you.

　　You may give them your love but not your thoughts,
　　For they have their own thoughts.
　　You may house their bodies but not their souls,
　　For their souls dwell in the house of tomorrow, which you
cannot visit, even in your dreams.
　　You may strive to be like them, but seek not to make
them like you.
　　For life goes not backward nor tarries with yesterday.

　　You are the bows from which your children as living
arrows are sent forth.
　　The archer sees the mark upon the path of the
infinite, and He bends you with His might that His arrows
may go swift and far.
　　Let your bending in the archer's hand be for gladness;
　　For even as He loves the arrow that flies, so He loves
the bow that is stable.

From THE PROPHET by Kahlil Gibran, copyright 1923 by Kahlil Gibran and renewed
1951 by Administrators C.T.A. of Kahlil Gibran Estate and Mary G. Gibran. Used by
permission of Alfred A. Knopf, a division of Random House, Inc.

CHAPTER 1

Why Is Parenting Someone Else's Child Different?

Many years ago, a friend asked me, not in jest, if I would take his biological teenage son into my home, raising him through the high school years. I asked him why he, an experienced foster parent, thought I could do any better with the boy than he could. "Because you don't have a *history* with him," he said.

Though we never went through with the arrangement, there was an element of wisdom in the statement of my friend — as I have since learned. Having had a hand in raising many children of other people, I now know that a fresh beginning can make a big difference in the end result. During difficult times with my own biological children, I often wished I knew someone who would trade with *me* — "just 'til we get through this problem, or stage; this is too hard!"

On the other hand, many prospective foster and adoptive parents have said to me, "Ann, I can't see any reason to attend all those classes. All *my* kids turned out OK. I must be doing something right!"

My answer? *Your* kids had nurturing, were wanted, were healthy, may have lived in a two-parent home, and received a good education. Not *one* child who is placed with you will have all that. And most of them will have had *none* of it. Although many people think, *"All you need is love,"* it just isn't true. Serious damage already may have been done by the time you get the child — even a 3-day-old child.

The research of Christopher Vaughan in *How Life Begins* (1996) reveals that babies can hear their mother's voice from the womb and can suffer from losses as brand-new infants. Many babies are affected by drugs and alcohol used during the mother's pregnancy, according to E.J.H. Mulder, et al., in their 2002 article "Prenatal Maternal Stress: Effects on Pregnancy and the (Unborn) Child." Other babies have the misfortune of sharing hormones and chemicals flowing through their mother's body, even if she wasn't "using." For example, a mother being abused by her spouse or partner has adrenaline surges far more often than most women. My own son, now a young adult, has suffered from chronic depression most of his life, and it may be due (at least in part) to my own depression during my pregnancy. Could he feel that? You bet! And I can tell you, even though he's mine, he has been a great challenge to parent. Imagine him being sent to live with you. You would have no idea why he is depressed. (By the way, I'm sure my son has found relating to me "challenging" as well!)

During my four decades of parenting, both biological and foster, I have supplemented my direct experience with a considerable amount of "book knowledge." Eager to learn more, I have signed up for continuing education classes, questioned doctors and psychologists, and networked with other foster and adoptive parents. It is my hope that this will become not only a "how to" manual but also a frequently used resource that you can refer back to when encountering each new challenge in raising your children. As you move through the material, perhaps you will find some things that "click."

In this chapter, let's begin by addressing issues that surround loss and attachment.

Special children

The title of this book has been almost a living thing. It ebbs and flows with my moods, or the needs of my audience, or the perspective I happen to be presenting this year. But this is a positive thing, because it tells me I'm not "locked in" to a particular view, that I continue to learn and grow, and that my research includes a lot more than attention deficit disorders, oppositional defiance, or learning disabilities. It contains the ingredients to help you build a working system for yourself.

My main goal in writing *Parenting Someone Else's Child* is to help you, the reader, be a good parent. That is, to help all the "special children" the best way we know how. Some authors, such as Dr. Stanley Turecki, call these children "difficult." Others use the term "special needs." Still others narrow their focus to specific disorders and syndromes, such as autism or ADD. I prefer to view them all as special children who need special parenting techniques — and who have special ways of learning and growing that we don't always understand.

My secondary goal is to make it easier for both you and your children to benefit from my suggestions by having them be adaptable to your own situation. Remember, don't expect to pick up someone else's system and have it fit your situation perfectly. Always *adapt* material and ideas to fit your *own* situation. In that way, you'll keep your family's uniqueness *and* have a system that works for each of you.

For years I focused on attention deficit disorders. At some point I began to realize that many of the things I was telling parents were common sense or would work with all different kinds of children, not just those with ADD. Second, I gradually began to realize what all the controversy was over ADD/ADHD. In the United States we were, indeed, experiencing an explosion in the ADD population, and we were trying to educate parents so they could get help in working with these children. But we were placing tremendous burdens on mental health providers, special education systems, school personnel, doctors, and the government. With expenses mounting, I began to worry that legislative limits might be triggered regarding the help that families could get. But an even bigger problem loomed. The public started to see the mushrooming diagnoses of ADD and ADHD — asking how all these diagnoses could be correct.

So I changed course and started looking at other causes of ADD symptoms. At two different seminars I was given lists of alternate causes and ADD "look-alikes." Then I ran across the work of Dr. Ruby K. Payne. In her book *A Framework for Understanding Poverty,* as well as in her workshops, she talks about behaviors that often arise out of poverty and other environmental circumstances. Most of those behaviors sounded exactly like the ones of the ADD children I knew! So, I thought, does any of this make sense? Does it matter *why* a child can't pay attention as much as it matters *how we help that child overcome the problem?*

Thus, my original seminar titled "How to Live Happily with ADD," was changed to "Living with Difficult Children." Next I tried "Managing Difficult Children." At this point, I feel more that these kids are all "special children" — and that what works for ADD also might work for others.

Who are "special children," after all? "Special" children are those who differ in significant ways from the rest of the population because of their medical conditions, birth circumstances, or family situation. Or they could be showing strange behaviors, learning problems, ways of coping, or some sort of disorder. There are still others who have simply been dealt a tough hand in life — and so are special. When I began to list some "special children" and their characteristics, I discovered that many of my techniques, indeed, are ways to work with *all* children.

Loss — and the five stages of grief

Many prospective foster and adoptive parents are surprised when seminar leaders talk about the losses the *parents* have experienced. But these losses must be dealt with before the adults can move ahead emotionally. Facing their losses also helps them understand their future children's losses *and* helps them work through the grieving process.

If you have never had children — and plan to adopt — you already have encountered the loss of your dreams and hopes for biological parenthood. In addition, you may have had to deal with the fact that you are infertile or sterile and incapable of creating new life. Perhaps you have suffered several miscarriages or even had children born who didn't survive long. Many childless couples have experienced disease or trauma that has rendered them infertile or sterile.

Grandparents who are raising their grandchildren often have to face the sad truth that their own child or children may have "failed" as parents. They also may be losing their retirement years together, along with the financial security they worked for. Finally, the reason they are raising their grandchildren may have actually broken the relationship between them and their child, or the disagreements between the two sets of parents may make the relationship very unpleasant.

Before entering the foster/adoptive system, it's important for these individuals and couples to work through the phases of their grief. These are discussed in detail in books and classes. An author often cited is Elisabeth Kubler-Ross. She describes five stages of grief, beginning with **denial**, the initial reaction people usually have when first confronted with loss.

Typical denial responses are recognized by familiar phrases, such as:

- "He can't be dead; I just saw him this morning."
- "I can't have cancer. I had a physical just four months ago and was fine."
- "The baby has to be alive; I just felt it kicking."

These are statements that show how difficult losses may be for people to accept — and their mind's attempt to shield their emotions.

In the case of children who are removed from their parents by a court, the children often deny that the parent did whatever he/she is accused of, even though it really happened. Or the children tell you it won't happen anymore, even though they know the parent has had many chances to change.

If you can, try to imagine the many losses these children experience. To name just a few, they include home, parents, siblings, friends, school, status, pets, clothing, prized possessions, routines, extended family, neighborhood, and so on. Now imagine, if you can, how empty and angry you would feel if I suddenly transported you to my house and told you to follow my rules, live with my children, care for my pets, and eat at my table. Imagine not being able to call home, check on your kids, feed the dog, see your friends, and go to work. I often wonder how any child survives the trauma of being removed from home. Yet many do and even learn to begin a new life with loving and caring parents, such as you.

The second stage of grieving a loss is described as **bargaining**. Many people begin to pray when the news sinks in — or even as they're in the process of losing a loved one. They'll say such things as, "Please, God, let him live. I'll do _____ if you do. Please don't let him die now."

Many foster children also "bargain." They can be heard saying things like:

- "Please don't blame my mommy. I was bad. If you let me go home, I'll be good, and she won't hurt me anymore."
- "If you let me go home, I'll take care of my little brother, and he won't have to stay by himself."
- "My Daddy says he will stop drinking if you send me back to him."

It's important to gently help a child through this stage, learning to face the reality of the situation. Although "imaginings" are part of the mental construct of such children, they aren't lying to you. They're going through the bargaining stage of their grief by escaping into their fantasy world where none of this is happening. The fantasy becomes reality to them.

After the bargaining stage, people usually enter an angry stage. In the depth of our **anger,** we may blame God, our spouse, the children, the "system," or even our parents. Such anger may be verbalized, acted out, or both. Children in foster care frequently break things, scream at their foster parents, and refuse to cooperate with those in authority — and find ways to secretly "get back" at anyone they think is to blame for their loss. This anger also will be addressed in other parts of the book, but it's an important element in the grieving process and shouldn't be denied. In addition, those who believe in God/the Supreme Being should know that temporary anger at God is normal and shouldn't add guilt to an already difficult situation. Even so-called saints in the Bible sometimes expressed anger at God.

The fourth stage of grieving is **depression**. A person is sad — or may even become clinically depressed — during this stage. In order to help children work through this stage, their anger, first of all, needs to be acknowledged. Their feelings should not be criticized, and the parent must be watchful for feelings to resurface at any time. Some adults attempt to soothe their own depression or anger after a significant loss by applying to adopt or foster a child — in an effort to fill the "hole in my heart" or their feelings of emptiness after the loss. Experienced social workers will delay licensing these people, suggesting a waiting period, to allow them to finish grieving before undertaking the challenge of a new child.

The last stage of grieving is **acceptance**. That is the only time individuals can truly say they have progressed through the entire process and begin to move on with their life. Children shouldn't be adopted until they have reached that stage, and parents shouldn't attempt to deny feelings (the child's *or* their own) during all the stages of grief and loss. It also should be recognized that people can go into and out of grief stages when a particular event or thought triggers this. Examples are experiencing "the first Christmas without him" ... or seeing a photo of a lost loved one ... or having someone bring up an event or idea connected with that person. These times gradually become less painful but still must be reckoned with.

Attachment

Much work is being done on **attachment** these days. Everyone who parents the children of others must deal with attachment issues. Parents may experience emotional attachment long before they see their child. Then when the baby is born, bonding and attachment can grow by a "give and take" between child and parents. They look lovingly into the baby's eyes and imprint its face on their mind. Baby cries, and they respond, taking care of its needs. The infant can recognize the smell and the taste of the mother's breast milk. The baby knows the sound of its mother's voice, even before it's born, and perhaps that of its father too. As more studies take place, amazing facts surface about the interaction between baby and parents, long before birth.

Many parents don't know that infants suffer losses when removed from their mother — and that such losses usually have a lasting effect on the children. In addition, children who have been in the foster care system (or who have been moved from parent to parent, friend to friend, relative to relative, caretaker to caretaker) experience a loss from every move.

I like to use a piece of tape as an illustration to my adult students. If I put the tape on your arm and tell you it represents the attachment you and your child have at birth, then pull it off, it hurts. And the longer it has been on, the more it hurts. But the next time I put it on you (or someone else), it doesn't attach quite so well. So if I pull it off, again, it will hurt less. And if I attach it to a third person's arm and pull it off, it hardly hurts at all. This is because it *did not attach* as well to the third person.

No one can predict the number of attachments a child can make, but everyone who works within the foster/adoptive system has seen the process. You have dreamed of receiving your child or children for months or even years, and when they arrive in your home, you welcome them with open arms. So why don't they look thrilled to be there? Why won't they return the love you offer them? Because they have usually suffered several moves or removals from significant people in their life and are subconsciously (or even consciously) afraid to attach again. The result of attachment, for them, is pain.

Other results stem from attachment problems. If children haven't had their needs satisfied as an infant, they might suffer attachment problems. If a parent or caretaker doesn't nurture and hold a baby enough, long-lasting deficits result. Young mothers who don't know this may prop a bottle and leave the infant alone or put the child in an infant seat for hours, instead of giving the child bodily contact. The child's emotional growth suffers, and the normal development of his/her ability to attach is stunted.

In addition, severely affected children may never develop a conscience, a sense of moral right and wrong, or the ability to see and identify with the pain of others (sometimes called empathy). They may have great difficulty forming relationships that last, such as sibling to sibling or husband to wife or even parent to child. As they grow, these children/adults go through friendship after friendship, marriage after marriage — or live with several different partners throughout life. Many of them also have a tremendous amount of underlying anger and depression, so they present major challenges to anyone attempting to parent them or relate to them. And some may never learn to trust others, for no one has ever satisfied their needs before, and expressing their needs may even have brought them pain.

Is there hope for these children? The painful, but true, answer is: not always. And one can't say, "All they need is love." For if the losses are numerous enough, and the deprivation is frequent enough, some never can find healing and wholeness.

Further, if children have never developed empathy or a conscience, they can't benefit from the type of discipline many parents use — a teaching model. If you have been taught that discipline should teach a lesson, then beware those children with an attachment problem. Why should they feel badly from having misbehaved? They can't empathize with your pain, they don't have a sense of guilt, and they have been hurt so much that they fear no pain you could possibly inflict on them. So it becomes a challenge to train them — and to find ways to stop unacceptable behaviors from recurring.

Many excellent books on attachment problems are available. But if you run across a child who actually has been clinically *diagnosed* as having an attachment disorder, be cautious. These children may never return the love or devotion you lavish on them. You may never get positive reinforcement for parenting them. You could spend many nights crying with or for them before they grow up. Indeed, sometimes even *after* that. There are a few extraordinary parents who can raise children like this — without receiving anything in return from the child. I have met some of them. But I am not one of them. When I look into a baby's eyes, I want that baby to look back. When I hug a teenager, I want a hug back, not limp arms and mere tolerance.

One of the attachment-affected children I know already has lived with four different men for about a year each, become pregnant by three of them, and married twice. About to deliver her third baby, she has let her mother take her first child, the second child lives with her biological father, and the third will be given up for adoption. At this writing, the young woman was only 24. How many other men will she live with? How many friends will she lose? How many children will she bear in an attempt to find love and acceptance? Her adoptive mother weeps ... and prays for her daughter to somehow learn to attach, to connect in a way that will finally bring her happiness and contentment.

This chapter is not meant to dissuade you from adopting. I only hope to help you face reality so that you can embark on this marvelous adventure with eyes wide open, knowing what you may be getting into. Some of you reading this book already have fostered, adopted, or taken in the children of friends and relatives. Thus, you don't need to be warned. You already have been experiencing both the joys and hurts of raising these special children, and you're looking for answers — or at least someone with whom to think through the questions. Keep reading!

CHAPTER 2

Special Needs

'Active child'   'Difficult child'
'ADHD child'   'Special needs child'
'FAS child'   'Autistic child'

It is said that most people will not move away from the stove until they feel the heat — or even get burned. So why would a parent want to move away from easy and comfortable responses to their children, away from their habits and beliefs, away from the way their parents did things? Only because something is not working! Perhaps they cannot get compliance from their child. Perhaps they can't seem to teach them anything. For teachers, perhaps it's because they aren't able to manage their "difficult children." Or, in the case of foster parents, perhaps it's because they're trying to parent the children of other people. So, as the saying goes, "If you want to change something, do something different."

* * *

What sort of child does this book discuss? Dr. Stanley Turecki defines these children in his book *The Difficult Child* (2000). To Turecki, any child outside the boundaries of "average," "normal," or "ordinary" might be described as "difficult." Perhaps *all* foster children fall into this category, and many adopted children do as well. The reasons? All have been separated from their family of origin, thereby suffering the virtually inevitable effects of loss and separation. Many are abused or neglected and have no concept of "normal." To be sure, some biological children also fit this description but usually for reasons other than the ones cited just above.

To begin the process of discovery — and learn whether you want to do foster care or raise someone else's child — you must throw out your former ideas about caring for and helping kids. You also must throw out your stereotypes and notions about the kids in our foster/adoptive systems. There is a *big* difference between "helping" and "enabling." While some of the children we see coming through the foster care network are "hopeless and helpless," others are jaded, damaged, angry, and defiant kids who have the potential to harm others. I have said it before, but I'll say it again: The goal of this book is not to discourage you but to enlighten you and assist you. If you can correctly assess your goals, assets, liabilities, and capabilities ... foster care or adoption should be a satisfying and immensely rewarding experience for you. A good match is the beginning of a wonderful placement, as well as the start of positive interaction between parents and child.

So let's dive into learning about parenting these "special children" — and get ready to do a bang-up job! And let's toss those *old notions and preconceptions* into the trash barrel.

Build a new 'house,' better suited to raising your special child.

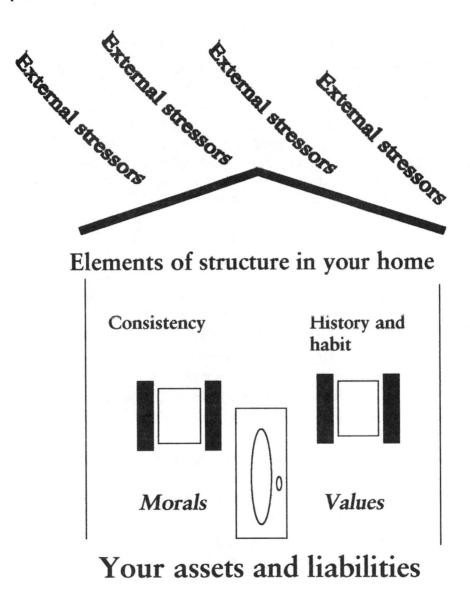

Elements of structure in your home

Consistency   History and habit

Morals   Values

Your assets and liabilities

Foster parents should learn to help doctors, teachers, and social workers in assessing the children who live in their home. Be wary, though, of trying to *diagnose!* Even if you aren't a doctor, you can make intelligent observations, document behaviors, and bring things to the attention of the professionals. The chart on page 31 titled "Assessment tools to help you" lists some similarities and differences between attachment disorders and other types of problems.

NOTE: One of the most asked-for handouts at the classes I teach is one that helps foster parents assess the symptoms and behaviors of their foster children. Again, see chart on page 31. I received this at a seminar I attended. I adapted and added to it, as my research progressed, including some of Dr. Ruby Payne's information in the last column. The original comes from attachment therapist Wanda Villet of Blanchard, Michigan. Villet works closely with the Michigan Foster and Adoptive Parent Association; she presents classes on attachment disorders to foster and adoptive parents.

There are *many* different causes for the behaviors our children manifest. The assessment chart on page 31 certainly is not all-inclusive, but it can help illustrate similarities and differences to assist in evaluating children. A thorough physical and psychological assessment must be done by qualified personnel before parents "decide" their child has some sort of disorder or syndrome. Many other factors can cause hyperactivity, inattention, daydreaming, and learning disabilities.

Perhaps the biggest reason for today's outcry regarding the over-diagnosis of ADD is because *parents* see their kids as hyperactive and see other forms of acting out, then *demand* such a diagnosis (and an instant cure). Daycare centers are insisting on children who can control themselves. Big schools and overcrowded classrooms mean that kids who daydream don't learn. Some doctors see patients every 10 minutes, specialize in ADHD, and don't really "know" the families they interact with. It may be difficult for them to determine all the reasons for a child's behaviors.

After studying ADD, ADHD, and related matters for years, I'm of the belief that it's all too easy for physicians to simply prescribe Ritalin — and sister medications like Adderall, Concerta, Welbutrin, and

Strattera — in such situations. However, if you have a good family doctor and go to him/her over a long period of time, he/she probably serves you very well. That's why the team concept, close follow-through, and careful monitoring are so important. Though we'll be discussing the team concept in greater depth later in the book, it basically involves *working with others* in your community to provide care and services for your child. Using the abilities of experts for the good of your child *and* support for you is sometimes the *only* way to be a good parent to a child with special needs. Sometimes the very reason you have the child is because his/her biological family couldn't deal with the child's needs. States and agencies are increasingly mandating that a wide variety of services be linked together for ongoing support for the family.

The listing below offers some of the most common reasons for hyperactivity or daydreaming. It should give parents food for thought and, I hope, slow down demands for an "instant cure." Here are some of these:

- Fetal alcohol syndrome (FAS).
- Closed head injury (in which internal bleeding and swelling have taken place, causing brain damage).
- Post-traumatic stress disorder.
- A parent's drug addiction (especially a pregnant mother).
- Poor hearing.
- Poor vision.
- Parasites, such as lice or pinworms.
- Hunger.
- Lack of sleep.
- Learning disorders.
- No motivation to learn.
- Nearly constant messages from the media (TV, radio, movies, billboards, newspapers, magazines ... even computers and video games).
- Children who seldom go outdoors or get exercise.
- Sexual, physical, or emotional abuse.
- Home environmental factors, including chaos and emotional conflict.
- "Parentified" children who are worried about parents and siblings (parentified children are those in a dysfunctional

family who take on the job of parenting siblings and may even parent the real parent or parents).

- Birth defects.
- A current stress or worry.
- *Parents who don't know what a normal, active child is!*

In addition, all parents — current and prospective foster, adoptive, *and* biological — are urged to read, talk, listen, attend classes, and learn in every possible way about parenting. Strange as it may sound, being "normal" is sometimes looked on as odd these days, and "everyone's" child seems to have a disorder or takes medications, so some parents almost seem to view dysfunction as a status indicator. How can we know what "normal" is? Observe. And learn.

For starters, you could volunteer to assist with a youth group at school or church. Chaperone a dance or attend a field trip with your child's class. Talk with parents of other children the age of your child. Learn the stages of development at each age. Observe groups of children playing. Visit your child's school, playground, gym class, and classroom. Go to the beach, watch, listen. Sit in the lobby at a college campus and "eavesdrop." Instead of hurrying through a mall, sit down with a cup of coffee and watch and listen to the children around you.

As the person who lives most closely with the child, you should be the one who's best able to observe behaviors. Learning to do this will make you a great asset to foster care, including your caseworker. Your doctor will learn to trust your observations and be able to better serve your child. You'll be able to take an active part in therapy and legal treatment of the child. Remember that while "a *little* knowledge is a dangerous thing," a parent with a considerable amount of hard-won knowledge is a much more effective parent.

Assessment tools to help you

ADD/ADHD	REACTIVE-ATTACHMENT DISORDER	BIPOLAR DISORDER	RAISED IN POVERTY
Had it since birth	From 3 years old on	From birth	Multi-generational
Lights matches from boredom; likes to watch fires	Wants to burn down your house	Varied reactions to fire; angry	Fire means total loss; no insurance
Short attention span, except when highly motivated	Short attention span only when bored	Attention span varies during manic and depressive phases	Apparent short attention span is learned behavior
Fifty percent inheritance rate or higher	Caused by life events	High rate of inheritance; often ADHD as a child	Different behavior patterns due to confusion
Motivational and organizational	Can mimic ADD	Can appear disorganized due to frenzied activity vs. lack of dependability	Disorganized due to transient lifestyle; constant crises; and verbal, not written, orientation
Extremely low self-esteem		Low self-esteem	Self-esteem depends on current environment
Friendly, over-stimulated	Superficially engaging	Self-oriented	Values ability to entertain group
Oblivious to detail			
Behavior programs work very well	Lack of conscience makes consequences ineffective	Will sometimes tolerate your control	Must have reason and motivation to respect controlling person
Tells lies, but sometimes fantasy makes story real to him/her			
May be bipolar; knows what is right, but refuses to do it			
Argumentative			

Foster or adopted children often come from homes of a class and background different from the foster home and have a different value system. As Dr. Payne has shown, this has a huge impact on the relationship and behaviors between the child and his/her new family.

They all are *someone else's children* entering *your* family system and trying to adjust. Many suffer from post-traumatic stress disorder (PTSD). Many are drug- or alcohol-affected, brain-damaged, or physically or mentally impaired. And the laws in most states say foster children cannot be disciplined by using corporal punishment of any kind.

In the language of adoption workers, "special needs" can mean age, race, inclusion of siblings, developmental or emotional disabilities, criminal history, sexual-abuse victim or perpetrator, or other reason the child is difficult to find a home for.

But even our biological children can be difficult if we don't know how to respond to their needs, while still addressing those of the rest of the family, as well as our own. That's how this came to be a book on parenting in general and not another one on attention deficit disorders alone.

It is my contention that nearly *all* children respond to high expectations, good structure, and liberal doses of both love and discipline. However, we're all so different that we interpret those things in different ways. Therefore, we need some kind of common ground and consistency with which we can work and successfully raise our children.

Systems run smoothly if the parts *function properly, the actions and reactions can be anticipated, and the people who interact know what to expect.* What that means is that human beings can adapt to almost any system — if there is *understanding, motivation, awareness, consistency, a support system, rewards, and a reasonable degree of predictability*. That way everyone can play by the rules, and everyone comes out a winner!

In teaching parents, I have learned that these six factors are basic ingredients that can spell s-u-c-c-e-s-s. There must be:

1. **Understanding** on your part of beliefs and habits the children may have had since they were very young.
2. **Motivation** to change, to grow, to learn before anything different and new can happen.
3. **Awareness** of roadblocks or personal "baggage."
4. **Consistency and persistence.**
5. A **support system** that is readily accessible to parents.

6. Some kinds of **rewards and reinforcements** for parents.

Now that we know what's needed, let's look at how to do it.

Understanding the children in your home, how they got into the foster/adoptive system, and what problems you and they might encounter are only the beginning. In this book I'm attempting to describe children's backgrounds, special needs, and reasons they may differ from your preconceptions of who and what they are. Of course, each child is an individual. None can be neatly tucked into a model and be completely understood. It's the job of each parent to learn and understand what makes his/her child tick. Only then can you move on to the rest of your job of parenting, adjusting your goals and methods for each child as you see the need, but remaining consistent and loving while you do.

Motivation is a key in all we attempt to do. When dealing with children, most people are quick to suggest ways to *punish* but take much longer to come up with ways to *motivate*. Both adults and children respond the same way. We work for our paychecks or for our beliefs and ideals or, perhaps, to satisfy our basic needs. Why would a child want to do the work of learning? Coming up with the answer to that will be one of your first goals.

Becoming **aware** of roadblocks or personal "baggage" is another beginning step. If you are going to parent successfully, you will need self-awareness — and to achieve that, some self-assessment is a must. Are you able to be consistent? Or do you, like me, have symptoms of ADHD and a basic difficulty with follow-through? Do you have a need to control? Do you have a great deal of self-doubt and insecurity? Are you obsessive or compulsive?

It can be helpful to sit down with a trusted friend or two (even your spouse, if that is your preference) and ask them how they assess your strengths and weaknesses. Then, when you begin to design the structure within which you'll work, you can insert some self-help elements. For a more detailed look at this self-assessment, see chart — and its preamble — in Chapter 4.

To be successful in what you do, there's also a need for **consistency** and **persistence.** In other words, find ways of developing patterns that work for you, then hang in there with the structures you establish with your children. Prospective foster or adoptive parents sometimes ask for — and receive — the advice of professionals, then don't heed it or follow through on it. There are occasions when the parents don't really understand *how* to do what the expert suggests. The way to create a well-designed plan and implement it is to *make the good design, try it, assess how well it works, and make the necessary changes.* Most inventions are refined and perfected many times before they can be marketed. Your management plan will be a *fluid system, frequently undergoing fine-tuning.*

Don't make the mistake of equating "fine-tuning"/making changes with inconsistency. When I first designed my "chore chart" (which we'll discuss later), it looked much as it does today. But, over several years, I've adjusted the chores for the age and ability of the children I've had in foster care, for their social life, for their absences (some visit their bio-parents as often as every weekend), and for the current needs of the household. I've done the same with children's allowances; the household budget; and my own schedule for work, play, and social activities. You have too without realizing it. I see it because I write everything down, then go back and look at it periodically. The *reason* I write things down is that some of my own weaknesses are a very poor memory, inconsistency, and lack of follow-through. The charts and reminder notes posted in my home help both my children *and me.* Design checks and balances in your system, do periodic reviews, and make adjustments. Neither you nor the children are the same today as yesterday. While you both will thrive on routine and predictability — and flounder on erratic and unclear expectations and constantly changing methods — change may still be necessary *in small doses*.

The goal is not to turn a spontaneous, exciting personality into a boring drudge or a precise, neat, predictable personality into a chaotic mess. You'll find your own level of comfort within a loose framework of consistency, balance, support, and success.

Which brings us to our last two points: **support system** and **rewards/reinforcements** for parents.

Later we'll discuss support systems at greater length. But let's say this now ... Each support system is different, but there are enough similarities that you can learn from the model. An important part of a social worker's job when assessing families is to find out whether they have support systems. For some of us, there are several extended family members close by. For others, it may be church people, a best friend, neighbors, adult children, or whoever would be there to help in an emergency — or with whom to celebrate successes. Anyone who encourages, listens, advises, or assists can be part of your support system. It's important to realize that parenting is not a single individual's responsibility, and parenting a difficult child calls for extra support. The African proverb, "It takes a village to raise a child," is particularly true for the special children we're parenting.

So ... what rewards are there in parenting such children? (If you don't know, then you're in trouble! Again, you may need to assess your situation.) Suffice it to say, the key is an internal *sense of satisfaction* in making a difference in the life of a child. Foster and adoptive parents who need a constant flood of external accolades, such as certificates for the wall, may end up very disappointed.

Outsiders often can tell if a parent is getting few rewards or little satisfaction because the parent frequently stops taking responsibility, neglects or ignores the child, or finds reasons to spend time away from home and parenting. Some physically or mentally impaired children are put into institutions by parents who are *unwilling* to deal with the complexities of parenting them. Some very young parents are *unable* to set aside their own needs and look first to the needs of their children. (A normal growth stage of most teens is a few years when they're very self-centered and see the world primarily through their eyes and seldom through the eyes of others.)

Foster and adoptive parents must undergo this self-assessment. Although some people think foster parents take children for the money, they haven't looked at reality. The "pay" is usually less than a dollar an hour. The responsibility is total. They live in a "fishbowl" where the agency, the neighbors, even strangers watch them nearly every moment. There is a vast array of restrictions. The child almost always costs more than the parents are reimbursed for! But here are some common reasons individuals give for wanting to parent:

- A child, in a sense, is an **extension of you**. If a child succeeds, you feel pride. If the child fails, you feel failure. A child may be able to take success even farther than you have.
- Perhaps **you cannot have your own** children.
- You may feel you have a "calling" or a **"ministry"** with children.
- You may feel that parenthood **fulfills a deep emotional or biological need in you.**
- You may be **a helping type** of person and derive your deepest satisfaction from parenting the children of others — who are unable to do so themselves.
- You may experience joy as a result of **molding and forming a child into something special and positive.**
- You may believe you can help **stop the cycle of failure and poverty** by offering a child from poverty other choices.
- Or maybe you simply **enjoy being with children,** and there are none in your home!

This discussion is continued in greater depth in Chapter 9, which is titled Motivation (Or, 'Why Should I?').

Parents of difficult children soon learn to take pleasure in small victories — and to feel successful when they see small changes. At times just helping to stop the constant conflict in a family is reward enough! My personal satisfaction has come to me in many forms. I'm extremely **proud** of my very **successful** two oldest biological children. I feel particularly **needed** by two of my adopted children. I take great pride and happiness in one of the adopted children, partly because it everyone thought she was "hopeless." My husband and I struggled for several years while raising a fine young lady — sort of a "rags to riches" story.

I believe that we have successfully intervened in the lives of many foster children — and in the lives of four adopted children, whom **no one else seemingly wanted. I love sharing,** via writing and teaching, what I have learned about parenting. *I like the compliments* I get from others … when they see a change in a difficult child. My husband needs little outside reinforcement, but I'm not the same person he is. There are some really tough days for parents. *It's nice to be noticed* and appreciated, at least once in a while!

When you foster or adopt, you may encounter a few other special problems. You may, for instance, take a child of a race different from yours. You will then be challenged by the need to help him/her know his/her heritage, and you may face prejudice and criticism from others. You might take a sibling group and, if you do, you'll be attempting to change an established pattern of behaviors that has evolved through the lives of the children. You may even engage in a power (and control) struggle with a child who has been the "parent" of the group, practically since birth. The age of your child will have a great impact on the degree of difficulty you have, as will your preferences. I, for one, *love to live with teenagers*, while friends of mine much prefer babies and toddlers. Remember, if babies are your "thing," don't take six of them and expect clear sailing when you have six teenagers in your house 10 years later!

Socrates had it right when he said, "Know thyself."

CHAPTER 3

The Impact of Social Class

Understanding your child's point of view

*"Children learn what they live" is a saying that summarizes this chapter. The formation of our very **being** starts as early as the nine months we spend in the uterus. Preferences and tolerances for noise levels, activity levels, colors, smells and other elements of our surroundings get started in infancy. Some parents consciously begin "forming" their children right away, while others are formed by default. But any time we attempt to train another person's child, we will have to deal with what is already imprinted — and how it may differ from our own vision.*

* * *

Few parents understand the impact that social class can have on raising other people's children. One's social class has a significant effect on one's values, morals and ethical system. Further, our individual tastes are formed as we grow in our environment, listen to those around us and are "steered" by our parents. Even young children already have learned to like and dislike clothing styles, foods, and forms of entertainment. One of my most vivid memories as a 7-year-old child comes from an issue of "taste."

When I was 4 years old, my family moved into a poor, Polish-Catholic neighborhood. My father had decided to return to medical school and learn a new specialty. We squeezed into a 1½-story post-World War II "bungalow" that had no basement, no garage, and no finished upstairs. Our family of six filled to capacity the two bedrooms on the main floor.

It is well-known that most Catholics don't endorse birth control. In addition, poor families have always had more children than the wealthy. In our little working-class neighborhood, my street was probably typical. More than 100 school-age children were living on my block alone! Nearly all of them were Catholic, as was my mother. Soon it was time for a major event in the life of a young Catholic: my first communion.

My paternal grandmother, who had always lived in wealth, had the values of the wealthy class. My mother, who grew up in a solid middle-class home, had great aspirations and married a doctor, who could elevate her social standing. She wanted all her children to make the step "up" to the so-called upper class, and she raised us accordingly. For my first communion my mother and grandmother chose a beautiful dotted-Swiss dress, with tiny lace edging on the collar, and shiny white patent-leather shoes. It was a "classic," and unlike any other dress on the block. *I cried.* All the other kids had rhinestones and glitter. Their shoes glittered, their dresses looked like wedding gowns, and they wore beautiful tiaras. My dress was *plain.* I had to wear *gloves.* My shoes had no *heels.* My rosary was made of *pearls,* not shiny cut glass beads, like theirs.

Your tastes, your values, and your background will likely determine your reaction to my "plight." For the wealthy class, good taste means subtlety, quiet elegance, and understatement. For the poor, on the other hand, lots of glamour, a beautiful shine, and a dress that stands out in a crowd prove to everyone that parents have given the best to their child. It makes both child and parent happy, and all the oohs and ahs of the crowd give the child a feeling of self-esteem and the parents a vision of success. And, to most children, glitter is gorgeous! Sometimes I've wondered if my status as a "wallflower" throughout my adolescence originated that day! The admiration of *my* parents could be won if I shrunk into the background; went unnoticed; and remained quiet, "behaving like a lady." The admiration of the parents of my friends was won if they made a great impression on the others present and acted like the "belle of the ball." And this is the way we begin to form our children's value systems.

Later, when my father finished medical school and went into private practice as a surgeon, we moved into a bigger house, attended different schools, and lived among people with middle-class values. And when I became a teenager, we "graduated" into the neighborhood of those who had money, changing our lifestyle, our furniture, our dress and recreational activities, becoming a true "nouveau riche" (newly wealthy) family. As if that weren't enough, we joined a country club, I was sent to a private girls' academy, and was enrolled in "charm school" to learn proper social graces. And, once again, I hated it! You see, it was too late for me. My values were already formed. I saw no reason to join the "stuck up" kids at the private schools; attend their cotillions; eat at their clubs; learn to play golf; and always, *always,* "act like a lady." I was, therefore, a constant embarrassment to my parents!

Now, in case you're wondering why I'm telling you my personal life story, it's to illustrate the reason for some of the attitudes other people's children bring into your home. In addition, the common question asked by foster parents and others who are doing this, "Why don't they want to be like me?" may be better explained if you look at it through the child's eyes.

The work of Dr. Ruby Payne, in showing us the differences among the classes (and the reasons for them) in the United States, should have a great impact on the foster care community. And a greater understanding of those differences should allow foster and adoptive parents to modify their demands on and expectations of children.

The past 30 years Dr. Payne has had firsthand experience with middle class, poverty, and wealth. Based on those experiences, as well as her observations about the three classes, she has put together the following 15-point chart on Hidden Rules Among Classes (1996). She explains:

"**Hidden rules** are the unspoken cues and habits of a group. Distinct cueing systems exist between and among groups and economic classes. Generally in the United States that notion is recognized for racial and ethnic groups, but not particularly for economic groups. There are many hidden rules to examine. The ones addressed here are those that have the most impact on achievement in schools and success in the workplace" (*A Framework for Understanding Poverty*, 3rd revised edition, 2003).

HIDDEN RULES AMONG CLASSES

	POVERTY	MIDDLE CLASS	WEALTH
POSSESSIONS	People.	Things.	One-of-a-kind objects, legacies, pedigrees.
MONEY	To be used, spent.	To be managed.	To be conserved, invested.
PERSONALITY	Is for entertainment. Sense of humor highly valued.	Is for acquisition and stability. Achievement highly valued.	Is for connections. Financial, political, social connections highly valued.
SOCIAL EMPHASIS	Social inclusion of people they like.	Emphasis on self-governance and self-sufficiency.	Emphasis on social exclusion.
FOOD	Key question: Did you have enough? Quantity important.	Key question: Did you like it? Quality important.	Key question: Was it presented well? Presentation important.
CLOTHING	Clothing valued for individual style and expression of personality.	Clothing valued for its quality and acceptance into norm of middle class. Label important.	Clothing valued for its artistic sense and expression. Designer important.
TIME	Present most important. Decisions made for moment based on feelings or survival.	Future most important. Decisions made against future ramifications.	Traditions and history most important. Decisions made partially on basis of tradition and decorum.
EDUCATION	Valued and revered as abstract but not as reality.	Crucial for climbing success ladder and making money.	Necessary tradition for making and maintaining connections.
DESTINY	Believes in fate. Cannot do much to mitigate chance.	Believes in choice. Can change future with good choices now.	Noblesse oblige.
LANGUAGE	Casual register. Language is about survival.	Formal register. Language is about negotiation.	Formal register. Language is about networking.
FAMILY STRUCTURE	Tends to be matriarchal.	Tends to be patriarchal.	Depends on who has money.
WORLD VIEW	Sees world in terms of local setting.	Sees world in terms of national setting.	Sees world in terms of international view.
LOVE	Love and acceptance conditional, based upon whether individual is liked.	Love and acceptance conditional and based largely upon achievement.	Love and acceptance conditional and related to social standing and connections.
DRIVING FORCES	Survival, relationships, entertainment.	Work, achievement.	Financial, political, social connections.

Also included in the succeeding pages are three eye-opening quizzes that will give you a deeper understanding, on a personal basis, of the hidden rules of economic class.

Score yourself in these survival quizzes.

COULD YOU SURVIVE … IN POVERTY?

Check each item that applies.

I know how to ...

_____ find the best rummage sales.

_____ locate grocery stores' garbage bins that have thrown-away food.

_____ bail someone out of jail.

_____ physically fight and defend myself.

_____ get a gun, even if I have a police record.

_____ keep my clothes from being stolen at the Laundromat.

_____ sniff out problems in a used car.

_____ live without a checking account.

_____ manage without electricity and a phone.

_____ entertain friends with just my personality and stories.

_____ get by when I don't have money to pay the bills.

_____ move in half a day.

_____ get and use food stamps.

_____ find free medical clinics.

_____ get around without a car or truck.

_____ use a knife as scissors.

Some of the things that had the greatest impact on me when I first heard about Dr. Payne's work were issues surrounding discipline, motivation, and behavior in school. In addition, I had been studying attention deficit disorders and training foster parents in how to manage ADHD children. I took a new look at the *behaviors* we were discussing. I soon realized that many are *related to class* and may not necessarily reflect a "disorder."

A wonderful thing about Dr. Payne's theories is the new skills we can learn to use in child management, teaching and raising our children, and advocating for them in the "middle class" system.

I no longer wonder why my well-formed discipline system doesn't *teach*. It's not a mystery to me why a *very intelligent* child won't get A's in school. I can cope with my foster child's demand for clothing that is "in" and his/her disdain for the second-hand shops I habitually buy from. And, most important, I no longer try to *change values*. Instead, I seek to *give choices,* along with reasons for them. I have learned to be creative when trying to manage a sibling group with a strong "parentified child" in control. I can relate to parents who feel uncomfortable in the social services offices and courtrooms, not to mention my home. I can boost self-esteem, instead of knocking it down, in subtle ways that enhance growth.

COULD YOU SURVIVE ... IN MIDDLE CLASS?

Check each item that applies.

I know how to ...

_____ get my children into Little League, piano lessons, and soccer.

_____ set a table properly.

_____ find stores that sell the clothing brands my family wears.

_____ order comfortably in a nice restaurant.

_____ use a credit card, checking account, and/or savings account.

_____ evaluate insurance: life, disability, 80/20 medical, homeowners, and personal-property.

_____ talk to my children about going to college.

_____ get the best interest rate on my car loan.

_____ explain the differences among the principal, interest, and escrow statements on my house payment.

_____ help my children with homework, and I don't hesitate to make a call if I need more information.

_____ decorate the house for each holiday.

_____ get a card at the public library.

_____ use most of the tools in the family's garage.

_____ repair items in my house almost immediately after they break, or I know a repair service and call it.

Middle- and upper-class people often attempt to foster or adopt older children who were raised in poverty. In addition, many Caucasian families are adopting interracially and cross-culturally. These well-meaning families learn how to do African Americans' hair, study Native American history, or travel to the Far East with their Oriental child. They apply all the "correct" disciplinary techniques while raising the child. But even though some things are going well, something is also wrong! For some reason, they don't achieve the results they had hoped for. What they don't understand is that they're attempting a deep-seated change of their child, who already has formed a value system and belief system, both of which are different from theirs.

First, if you understand children's developmental stages, you know that most of a child's personality is formed very early — with some beginnings even while in the uterus. Then, the longer a child stays with his/her biological family, the more firmly the family world-view is a part of that child's psyche. What most people are *not* aware of is that different socioeconomic classes of people teach their children different values. Further, children learn to survive in the world they are in as babies. And finally, foster children have already had role models to follow by imitation, long before you get them.

You may remember that earlier we talked about motivation. What motivation would foster children have to "change" their entire belief system? Would they view a foster parent as more intelligent than their own parent? Would they cooperate with someone who indicated to them that their own beliefs were "wrong" and the new beliefs were "right"? In most cases, the answers are obvious. Therefore, we should start at the beginning and do an **assessment**. You will need to know what value system the child has, then work within the framework of *that* system, *not your own!*

In her *Framework* book Dr. Payne explains the differences in basic behaviors and belief systems between most children raised in poverty and most children raised in middle-class and wealthy families. These differences extend far beyond the amount of money they have. Their outlook on survival, basic needs, religion, sex, right and wrong, discipline, and many other factors is very different.

COULD YOU SURVIVE ... IN WEALTH?

Check each item that applies.

I ...

_____ can read a menu in French, English, and another language.

_____ have several favorite restaurants in different countries around the world.

_____ know how to hire a professional decorator to help "dress up" my home for the holidays.

_____ can name my preferred financial advisor, lawyer, designer, hairdresser, and domestic-employment service.

_____ have at least two homes that are staffed and maintained.

_____ know how to ensure confidentiality and loyalty with domestic staff.

_____ use two or three "screens" that keep people whom I don't wish to see away from me.

_____ fly in my own plane or the company plane.

_____ know how to enroll my children in the preferred private schools.

_____ am on the board of at least two charities.

_____ know the hidden rules of the Junior League.

_____ support or buy the work of a particular artist.

_____ know how to read a corporate balance sheet and analyze my own financial statements.

_____ know how to host parties that "key" people attend.

Thus, according to Dr. Payne, your attempt to use discipline to "teach" your children — or your attempt to teach the children to "save for the future" and make a budget — may be in vain. Instead, you must find ways to motivate them to learn your "secrets" or "*hidden rules*" *for succeeding in the adult world and the workplace.*

> **Scoring your quizzes:**
> If you fall mostly in the middle class, the assumption is that everyone knows these things. However, if you did not know many of the items for the other classes, the exercise points out how many of the hidden rules are taken for granted by a particular class, which assumes they are a given for everyone. They aren't.

We can address a few of these differences here, but an in-depth study would be worthwhile for many foster parents. The major implications to discuss are the following facts:

1. Since foster parents are shown how to use discipline as a teaching tool they should know that children from poverty look at it as "penance" and not a reason to change their behavior.

2. Since many middle-class families believe in saving money for future emergencies and needs, they should know that children raised in poverty view every minute of every day as a time of emergency and *immediate* needs. Thus, money is to be spent *now*.

3. Many symptoms of ADHD appear in children raised in large cities, if they have lived in ghettos or dangerous neighborhoods. The hyperactive behavior, the wandering attention, and many other traits are survival mechanisms they develop to ensure their personal safety in a place where they must be on the alert at all times. They may *not* have ADHD and do *not* need medication to calm them down!

4. Issues of respect, status, authority, and safety all differ among the classes. Types of learning environments, styles of learning, and ability to understand the written word vary greatly.

5. The poor live in a matriarchal society. Middle-class families are more oriented toward a patriarchal one, and the rich see little difference between the status of men and women (or in their rights and authority) because it depends largely on who has the money.

Many other differences appear when we examine children from different classes and environments. These all affect the ability of foster parents to succeed in raising the children they care for. And this is the main reason this book addresses management of *all* children, not just those with ADHD.

Four points regarding the suggestions that follow:

- All hyperactive children should respond to these techniques.
- All angry children would benefit from these methods.
- All inattentive children could learn more easily with these supports.
- All chaotic and uncontrolled households would benefit from more structure and routine.

Therefore, we shall address many of the most frustrating situations all parents face, then attempt to give suggestions for ways to deal with them.

 *Offer choices*

Parents must look at more than simply following an outline from a book in order to raise their child.

EVERY home is different, every personality is different, and all methods will not work for all parents. It is necessary to find your comfort level and put together a program that suits you and your children.

Creativity will be your greatest asset. Challenge yourself to adapt these ideas, not copy them.

The *biological family* of children determines many factors before they ever enter your home. *Genetics, of course,* plays a great role in such factors as intelligence, race, appearance, some mental illnesses, and temperament.

In addition, there's a growing body of research in the field of *environmental factors* and their impact on children, even in the mother's womb. As first addressed in Chapter 1, recent research in behavioral science reveals that a pregnant woman's stress level is transmitted to the growing fetus. "[The stress] results in early programming of brain functions with permanent changes in [hormone production] and behavior in the offspring," report E.J.H. Mulder, et al., in a 2002 article titled "Prenatal Maternal Stress: Effects on Pregnancy and the (Unborn) Child." Physical changes take place in the growing baby, and excessive amounts of chemicals released by stress enter its bloodstream.

According to B.R.H. Van den Bergh in a 1990 article titled "The Influence of Maternal Emotions During Pregnancy on Fetal and Neonatal Behavior," "Fetuses of women with high anxiety tended to be more active than fetuses of women with low anxiety. The prenatal influence was reflected in neonatal behavior."

After the baby is born, the continuation of a chaotic environment adds to those receptors and reinforces chemical reactions. Eventually, many such children become a "problem" in school and society. We currently label them as "Oppositional Defiant" or "Attention Deficit Disordered" or "Conduct Disordered." Scientists are tracing the origins of these behaviors all the way back to the womb! Animal studies have shown this for many years, but only recently have scientists been able to verify them with human studies. They can find chemicals in babies' blood and document behavior, both pre- and postnatally, via ultrasound and other monitoring devices. Such factors as a pregnant mother's drug addiction, alcoholism, depression, nutrition, and lifestyle have been found to affect children before and soon after birth. Life's experiences — from birth to a toddler's home life on into the school years — do their additional work, molding and carving out differences in us as we grow.

We already have discussed **training** as a third major factor in the full scope of the personality. Many parents are consciously aware that they are forming values and morals in their children, but some are not. They simply raise their children as their parents raised them, and the results are too often predictable!

Parents also are aware that differences can result in **conflict**. If you ask most parents, they'll tell you they want their children to marry someone from a similar background and that "mixed marriages," by most standards, are difficult. They mean that whether it's partners from different countries, races, religions, social levels, or other major differences ... conflict and struggle could ensue as the new family's lifestyle is formed.

Well ... *Parenting Someone Else's Child* is just this kind of "mixed marriage"!

"I'm not like you" is a refrain heard frequently by parents of teenagers, foster children, biracial children, and some adopted children. And they're right! In most cases, they are *not* like you or me. They are

unique. Yes, our biological children also are unique but usually not in such extreme ways. Perhaps the best way to begin working with children is to acknowledge this fact, both for you and the child. When appropriate, I even discuss the differences in detail with new foster children in my home. It's a good way to establish a relationship based on mutual respect and understanding.

In my experience the next statement out of a foster child's mouth often has been, "Why should I have to be like you — or do it your way? My way is fine with me. If people won't accept me the way I am, then I don't need them."

My answer? Well, it depends on my relationship with the children, the length of time they have lived with me and their own level of understanding. You can discuss the issue of following the rules in your home while they are there — and the rules in their own home when they are there. Most of them understand how to follow different sets of rules. They act differently at home than with their peers at school. They behave differently on the street with friends than they do in the company of adults or parents. The two of you also might be able to examine the way they act, then determine if some of those actions might have led to them being in your home in the first place. (But be very careful here about mentioning anything about how their *parents* acted. That's a surefire way to ignite defenses and anger.)

You could even joke with them about not wanting everyone to be alike, because it would be a boring world. But, in my opinion, that makes light of a subject that is not a light one. This isn't the first time they have asked the question "Why should I have to act like you do?" They have undoubtedly been criticized before. They may honestly want some sort of explanation. Or they may be expressing a long-standing resentment.

The key here, I believe, is to show them the importance of context. As discussed above, behaviors that are appropriate in one place are not necessarily appropriate another place. How one acts at a football game is different from how one acts in a church, synagogue, or mosque. That doesn't mean one's values change, just because one's setting changes, but it does mean that respect is shown for that new setting — such as a foster home — and for those who establish the ground rules in that new setting.

By the way, never underestimate the value of "think time." Stopping the conversation at a teachable moment helps them think about it and not gloss over the nugget you have offered. Later you can explain, if the time seems right. For now, though, you have offered some food for thought, tied it in with power and control (which most of them don't have), and defused a potential conflict in your home.

Respect

Trying to change value systems is a trap many foster parents fall into. Any attempt to change a person's value system could be seen as an insult to their current one. It isn't by force that these things change, but rather by respect, example, encouragement, and enlightenment. Your value system is a personal thing, formed by only you. You make the decisions about your beliefs and behaviors based on what is shown you and what you have experienced. You may have had (or still have) a role model or mentor whom you imitate. You may have been *forced* to go to religious classes or a certain school, but you *chose* whether to accept what was presented to you.

Remember your adolescence? It was a time of questioning, rebellion, and search. You were forming your value system as you emerged into adulthood. You had been shown, taught, even subjected to a number of things that gave you a basis for a value system. Then you chose to either imitate and absorb those things — or reject them and rebel against them. Many children say, "I'll never be like my [parent]. I'll never do ..." Some follow through on that, while most don't. Those who don't are probably those who haven't been shown another way; *they haven't learned to make conscious choices about how they lead their life.*

You can make conscious decisions to *try* to change children's value system, no matter how old they are. But you can't *do* it by force. And the older the child, the more important this is to recognize. Exposing infants and toddlers to the things you hope they'll absorb is one thing; it isn't too difficult. But try to make a 14-year-old go somewhere with the family because you want them to absorb something educational or cultural! You certainly *can* force them to *go.* But they almost certainly won't be absorbing what you're hoping they will.

Dr. Payne's work may give us the best answer of all. The answer is that you want to give your children (especially teens) *choices* that will afford them more freedom, more power, and more control over their own life. A discussion of the "hidden rules" in society, the secret ways to get ahead, and the amount of control it will give them in their everyday life and their future just may be the best answer of all.

Which brings us to another method of working at change: being a role model.

Be a role model

Being, or finding, a **role model** for a child is one of the most important things you can do to put any kind of change into practice. During the last few years of my career as a foster parent, virtually all the teenage boys and girls who lived here expressed something very important to me: *They admire my husband and have a great deal of respect for him.* For boys, that means they will always carry with them the image of the kind of man people look up to — and perhaps what they would like to be. For girls, this image will remain with them as they search for a mate or gain understanding of the way a man should treat a woman.

Role models have numerous other implications for young people. They might believe they could be like their role model if they did what the person had to do to get where they are. They might decide to go to college or enter a life of service (public servant, medical career, teaching). They may have never known anyone with a skilled trade (tool and die, electrician) and find such a vocation fascinating or desirable. A girl might learn how to be a good mother ... a boy, how to be a good father.

Some of the things our children have learned and imitated have amazed us. One of our adopted sons took up the sport of dog training, taking his retriever to competitions and winning ribbons, as well as breeding the dog. An adopted daughter has learned to budget and is proud of the many money-saving things she does every day. One son learned to express himself well in writing, switching from an engineering program in college to a business communications career that has taken him all over the world and brought immense financial success. A boy from the ghetto decided to improve his grammar in order to get a better job. He got a good job the day he graduated from high school. At this writing he was holding that position.

None of this was forced or coerced onto these children. Though these options were presented and "lived" by role models, they were chosen freely. When my husband and I presented these things, we assisted the children in learning them, but we never could have forced them to make the decisions they did — to internalize them and *keep* them for themselves.

At the front of this book I included "On Children" by Kahlil Gibran, the great Lebanese poet of the early 20th century. He says, "Your children are not your children. ... They come through you but not from you, [a]nd though they are with you yet they belong not to you. ... You are the bows from which your children as living arrows are sent forth."

Even very young children resist coercion and pressure. When our little granddaughters visit us they usually ask to "help" with dishes or housework. I set them up with a pan of water and some plastic dishes, and let them go to work. But if I try to make them do it, when they're not in the mood, I invariably encounter resistance. That isn't to say that I have our children do the cleaning only when they "feel like it." They soon learn, when they live here, that the work must be done before play — and that in this regard it matters little how they feel! But, while I train them, I must bear in mind that regular cleaning chores may not fit in with their own value system.

 *Assist*

I also know that teaching a child to do a task requires that I assist them, not simply order it done. And why the discussion of tasks at this point? Because the level of cleanliness in one's home, the amount of time spent on this, and even who does it and how it's done are all elements of a *value system.*

Praise and uplift

Never forget to *praise* and *uplift* a child. Children who come from families other than our own, with the possible exception of infants, probably have self-esteem issues, including low self-confidence. They may have been verbally or physically abused. They may have been forcibly removed from their own families (or even voluntarily given up) and feel worthless. Those two words are so important to raising any child they must be highlighted!

Reward

And, finally, why would a child want to *keep* something he/she has learned from you? *Because there's a reward for doing it.* Does that mean children get a blue ribbon because they learned to eat with a fork? No, nor does it mean the parent always supplies the reward. We continue to do things because of *positive reinforcement.* Perhaps, as with getting a job, we now have a steady paycheck. Perhaps, by getting good grades, we become the first person in our family to graduate. Perhaps, by taking part in competition, our dog wins a blue ribbon, which is the first thing we ever did that caused anyone to admire us. So, parents, remember that where there's no reward, there will likely be no change! If you need to supply the reward in the beginning, do it. The external rewards will follow, as will the *internal self-esteem.*

Be creative in your rewards. Most parents don't seem to run out of ideas for punishment, but if you sit down and try to list rewards that are appropriate for different accomplishments, you may be hard-pressed to come up with a list. Praise, time spent with a child, special privileges, dessert, an outing with you, and many other things that don't cost money are wonderful rewards. My grandchildren respond very well to the promise of "snuggle time," which is when we sit on the couch with a lap blanket, and I just hold them and sometimes read to them. We also may talk, or they may be allowed to fall asleep on my lap for naptime or bedtime. They love every minute of it. Many moms (and dads) either don't *have* the time to do it, or don't *take* the time to do it.

These principles work for nearly all children. And ... surprise ... they work for adults too! Wives (and husbands), try offering "snuggle time" to your spouse to thank him/her for something he/she has done for you. Nagging and begging for little jobs around the house won't get you as far! So ... here's to improved home lives for us all!

Speaking of mothers, children raised in poverty often give their foster mom a hard time. First, the foster mother must understand that the children's relationships with parents in *their* home may be very different from *the foster mother's* expectations and experiences. In poverty, children often have a single mom raising them, along with an absent father. The way in which a boy's father related to his mother will have had a great influence on the way he relates, not only to his own mother, but also to all adult women in authority. Foster parents may be surprised to see that even very young children seem determined to run their own life and lack respect for adults. So many issues are involved in this phenomenon it can be difficult to determine how to cope with it.

Children may be angry with their mother because they are in foster or adoptive homes at all. They may believe that their parents either caused them to be removed or failed to protect them from being removed. They may then transfer this anger onto the "mother figure" in their new home.

Another reason for lack of respect can be that their own parents didn't parent them effectively, and they have no reason to trust different adults to do any better.

Third, an older sibling who has "parented" younger siblings as long as he/she can remember will find it very difficult to allow someone else to parent either the "parentified child" himself/herself *or* the younger siblings.

In addition, foster/adoptive parents must learn new rules about gaining respect from children from other types of backgrounds than their own. Children raised in poverty seldom respect you for the role you play, such as parent, teacher, police officer, or other authority figure. Instead, they respect you because you show respect for them and prove yourself loyal, worthy of respect in your own right, and don't take yourself too seriously. As Dr. Payne has shown in her book on understanding poverty, *relationships are everything* to these young people. If you're able to establish a relationship with them, gaining their loyalty and trust, there should be few discipline problems.

These children observe carefully when they enter your home. They see how adults treat other adults. They see how the other children in the home treat the adults. They see how the adults treat the other children. All this happens during their "honeymoon" period in the new home. When they have established all the facts and rules in their own mind, they'll start playing the game. Experienced foster parents often term this "the end of the honeymoon." This is when the new children begin to test the parents. They'll drop the pretenses and guest-like behaviors and act like their true self. It is then that the struggle for *power and control* begins. One can only hope that the foster parents have been clear in their expectations. This is why social workers ask foster parents to come up with clear foster home rules *before the placement* — and cringe when the new foster parent says, "Oh, we'll figure out the rules when the time comes." By then it will be too late!

When children move into a new home, a new neighborhood, and a new school district, they face many challenges. If the children also move into a new social class, the job of fitting in may be nearly impossible. For most children, it's crucial to be accepted by peers and fit in with the other children, no matter what their age. The effects of criticism, cruelty, and ostracism by peers are well-documented. Most foster children are automatically *outside the "in crowd"* simply because they're "foster." And it's not just peers. There's a stigma, even prejudice, by the parents of classmates that they are there because they're "bad" or come from a "bad" family. This is added to the questionable distinction of being "the new kid" in school — and maybe even looking different from the others.

Therefore, an effort should be made to prepare foster children before sending them to school. A foster parent may want to observe how the children in the school dress. Parents may want to visit the school or take the children for a look-see before enrolling them. This can give children a chance to think about how they will need to look or act to be accepted. Other children in the family might want to advocate for the child, but this shouldn't be forced. At least, the foster or adoptive parent should meet the child's teachers and tell them something positive about the child prior to sending him/her to class. This will help build a positive image in the thinking of the teachers, along with an accepting attitude.

Children, especially teens, may well enter their new school with an "attitude." This is a defense mechanism, and foster parents should talk to them about it prior to sending them. There is usually real fear in the children in such situations, and they will use the "attitude" in their new school for self-defense. Ideally, the foster parent will have a few suggestions — or at least open a discussion about "attitude" with the child. Especially in the beginning it's important for the foster parent to have frequent, though relatively inconspicuous, contact with school officials. Asking the student how it's going seldom provides sufficient data. Students also may be attempting to impress their foster parents and won't likely want to reveal failure or weakness away from home. Of course, a "hovering mommy" is not the answer either! Instead, the parents should attempt to work discreetly with school personnel to smooth things out and find ways to empower the children themselves.

All human beings want power and control over their own destiny. But, while waiting for "destiny," they want to be able to control their own circumstances. This real or imagined control is stripped from a child in foster care when the first contact with the court or Child Protective Services occurs. Children are taken from their home, and everything that was familiar is left behind. Pets, parents, friends, neighborhood are gone. They are brought to a new home and told to stay. Many get no contact with their bio-parents (or anyone else familiar) for days or even weeks. In extreme cases, a few never see their parents again and are made available for adoption. Even tiny babies react to these losses. Young children feel helpless and often hopeless. And older children or teens frequently express anger and resentment through misbehaving or carrying a "chip on their shoulder."

I have tried to make it a practice to find ways to help a child feel some sort of *control* over his/her life. This applies to your own child or to any other child you deal with.

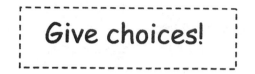

Give choices!

There are a hundred and one things you can let children choose in a day! They can choose their clothing, choose their breakfast food, and choose their hairstyle. They can choose a TV station, an activity, or a story to be read to them.

All these things are great rewards for good behavior! Many of these are things children think are rights. When I have a particularly difficult child to discipline, I find a time to sit down with him/her and make lists of "rights" and "privileges." All these choices are *not* rights. This may be a good time to list some rights and privileges and get our kids thinking about what they really do *have*. It's sort of a "heads-up" for kids, encouraging them to start thinking about what they can *lose* when they disobey rules. Many of the items below involve older kids in particular. I'm listing a few, just to get you started. Be creative!

Rights	Privileges
Shelter	Color and décor of bedroom
Food	What, when, and where
Clothing	Brand, style, color
Medical care	See doctor alone, braces, contacts
Privacy while dressing, bathing	Privacy while doing *anything* else
Parental protection	Advice, affection, attention
A safe and healthy environment	A place to bring friends, creature comforts, air conditioning or fan
An education	School of choice, help with homework, advocacy when problems arise
Allowance (if in foster care)	Any amount beyond personal *needs*
	A job, transportation
	Time with any individual
	Choices (channels, colors, foods, etc.)
	TV, recreation, games, movies, junk food, desserts, boom box with tapes or CDs, computer, etc.

You could expand this chart greatly. But the important point is that children — especially older children — need to understand when they're receiving something extra and when they're receiving a basic right. The chart could be developed by using an individual's tastes and preferences in the right-hand column, or it could be generic.

But back to the topic of choices ... Giving kids choices is empowering to them. The dictatorial view that "might makes right" or some other controlling force has ruled the life of many a kid. They also may have been abused, which strips them of all feelings of power and control. Therefore, they need to know when *they* are controlling what they do ... or what they get. Many of them also are very concrete in their thinking. So you must spell it out for them. Point out that they are *choosing* classes in their schedule, titles of books, colors, and outfits to wear. And *remind them that they are making choices about how to behave and how to react to others.*

So many kids who have come through my home have made the statement "He made me mad, so I ..." that it deserves attention here. Most of these children haven't been taught how to understand their emotions or how to control them. They also don't know they *have control over them!*

It helps children to have a picture of various emotions to refer to. You can draw a happy face, a sad one, a mad one, and a glad one. These can be expanded upon for older children. But talk with your children about how their body and mind feel when they're experiencing strong emotions, then have them practice telling you how they're feeling. Emphasize that *they* are in control over their feelings, and that no one can *make* them *do* anything. Also point out that it takes far more strength to turn and walk away than to fight or curse or have any sort of physical reaction when they're angry. In fact, getting a reaction may be just what the instigators want. Walking away deprives them of that satisfaction.

Further, be sure they remember that they have a choice when you ask them to stop and think about something they're about to do (or not do). I try to give time and space, telling my children the alternatives. An example might be: "You have five minutes to decide whether you're going with me or not. I will wait in the car for you to make up your mind. If you don't come, you will lose all phone privileges for a week." By stating the two alternatives (go or don't go), using a matter-of-fact tone of voice, and turning to walk away, you avoid conflict and resistance. You simply give the young person time to cool down, to think of the consequences, and to decide. There is no fight or argument.

The effects of being in foster care or being adopted are too numerous and complex to discuss at length. But some of the more common effects fall under "common sense." Children may feel angry or powerless. Children may feel they have been rejected by their birth parents. They may feel inadequate, lonely, sad, or relieved. If they're relocated a lot, they may develop an attachment disorder. If they spend a long time in foster care, they may become "systems wise" and learn how to get around the system that put them there.

Children who are in your home because of neglect or abuse may have strange mannerisms, including hypervigilance, hyperactivity, n numerous adaptive behaviors, fear of abandonment and unreasonable fears. They may have psychosomatic illnesses, crave attention, or lack trust. Children who have been delinquent may have no regard for laws or police. Other children learn how to "charm and disarm" you and are *too* sweet and compliant.

Some children in your home may have learning disabilities or emotional problems, requiring them to be in special education at school. They also may have failed one or more grades and have been held back. Much of that is due to frequent moves. Other children assume an "Oh, poor me!" attitude, while still others pay attention and learn from their situation.

There are far too many reports of abuse in foster homes, and (of course) good foster and adoptive parents look down on this. But nearly all children in the care of others who aren't in their own home show some signs of "wear and tear." These damaged kids may appear to be "normal" on the outside, but you can be sure they're hurting inside.

Good effects of being in your care may include:
- Improvement in grades.
- Improvement in health and personal hygiene.
- Improvement in habit and routine.
- Improvement in self-confidence.
- The ability to set goals and achieve them.
- Increased self-help skills.
- Independent-living skills.
- Survival skills.

Young people can learn coping methods from you; get psychotherapy or medication from you; and observe the way you live, giving them a choice as to how they will live when they are grown.

The class a child is raised in — and all the accompanying values, ideas, and attitudes — make a huge difference in how a child lives and grows into adulthood. Not long before his death Martin Luther King Jr. recalled that some of the most vicious racism he ever encountered was in 1966 in Cicero, Illinois, a middle-class suburb of Chicago. As Dr. King and other peaceful demonstrators walked through Cicero to protest housing practices, they were pelted with rocks, bottles, and racial epithets the likes of which King and his followers had seldom experienced. Who was hurling most of the hurtful objects and hateful words? ***Children who hadn't yet reached their teens.***

Where did these children learn such hatred? One can only imagine.

For better or worse, children learn what they live with. As stated earlier, values from an early age run deep. Such values are "in the bones" of children. Foster and adoptive parents have a great opportunity to present, through word *and* deed, a positive way of life to the special children who come to live under their roof.

But no one ever said it would be easy.

CHAPTER 4

What Are Your Strengths and Weaknesses?

*I have been attending workshops and continuing education seminars for at least 25 years. In addition to that, I have a bachelor's and a master's degree. Many of those classes are so long forgotten I can't even tell you what they were about! But there was a two-day seminar I attended, after the first few years of fostering, that I never forgot. The seminar addressed the reasons we decide to foster or adopt — to raise **other people's children.** In it, we examined our own strengths and weaknesses, and my self-concept was turned upside down. Things I had previously thought of as character flaws turned out to be incredible assets and strengths to be used in my new career as a foster parent!*

* * *

Some people kind of fall into raising someone else's child. Others make deliberate efforts to become licensed foster or adoptive parents. Still others go to court for legal guardianships. Whatever way you came to be the parent of children not born to you, you must know it isn't the same as raising your biological children. Many children coming to you have special needs. These may be mild or severe. They may be physical or emotional. Or both. In any case, you probably have some special skills to use when dealing with these children, or you would not have them at all!

During a licensing interview, prospective foster and adoptive parents are asked why they want to become licensed. Answers vary from emotional and touching reasons to practical ones to absurd misconceptions to reflective responses. By now you have read enough in this book to know that you will *not* be getting "a playmate for my toddler" ... or "a teenager who will keep me company when I'm lonely" ... or "someone to replace the child I lost." Each child is unique, but most who come into your home will need *you* and, for the most part, will not be satisfying *your* needs. There are rewards, to be sure, but they don't tend to be the ones you expect.

It may surprise you to know that all foster parents don't need to be nurturing in the way that calls for hugs and cuddles, kisses and warm soup in the winter! Many children can't tolerate touch at all. Others don't want affection from someone who isn't their own mother or father. Some situations call for strictness, structure, "tough love," and firm commands.

So ... what is it about you that will help you in this downright tough endeavor? First, remember that we discussed the way foster parents specialize in certain types of children? Imagine a sweet, petite, soft-spoken, and timid young woman who had lived in a nice suburban home all her life trying to parent a tough 17-year-old delinquent from the streets of the inner city. She *might* be able to command respect. But then again, it might be easier for a strong, outspoken, no-nonsense single woman (who had lived through some very tough times herself) to understand and deal with the same teenager, who could be male or female. (Often girls are more difficult than boys to parent!) All this isn't to say you must put yourself into a stereotypical role and behave in a certain way to take teens into your home. It's only meant to give you a picture of possibilities.

Perhaps you want to bring infants into foster care. You must be nurturing, selfless, willing to get up in the night, able to detach, and willing to take them to a doctor for their well-baby checkups.

Perhaps you want to run a group home for delinquent teens. You had better have a strong ego, good structure, a take-charge style, and no fear at all! (At least none that shows.) Shall I say "controlling"?! Well, try it once and learn how they seem to gang up together in a "them against you" manner! One teen is out of control? Perhaps you could deal with it, *if all the others didn't join in, take sides, and add to the chaos!* So you've been told you are controlling? This is not good in a job where you need to be a team player. But hey, you might make a great parent in a group home!

Perhaps you have an eye for detail that drives some co-workers nuts, but you have fun tracking sports statistics, gas mileage on your car, and the family's finances. A medically fragile child visits numerous specialists, requires many types of medications and treatments — and depends on absolutely accurate recordkeeping. You also may be reimbursed for mileage to medical offices, so you must be consistent with your records.

Perhaps you're inclined to be "obsessive-compulsive" and like everything planned out and orderly. You may be the perfect parent of a child who can't live without serious structure, excellent routine, and total predictability. Are you a peacemaker, even seeing positives in conflict? Can you seemingly get along with everybody? Then you'll be great at working with a child's bio-family, as well as a wraparound team.

Even though you aren't a lawyer, are you fascinated with the ins and outs of the legal system? Are you a stickler for knowing procedures and following them? Perhaps your child needs a stern advocate for his/her special education program, along with a well-planned program of services from the school system. You will know what's available *and* how to implement it. You also will know the child's rights and the limitations of the school system.

Are you a patient teacher with young children? Do you love to get on the floor and play with toddlers and other youngsters? Friends may have criticized you in the past for acting "childish," but "child*like*" adults who love kids are needed desperately by many special children out there. They may never have had a parent's attention. Or they may be behind in intellectual or motor development, and they simply need to take time to play. You will both have tons of fun!

I think you may be starting to see — as I did in my own life — how liabilities in the formal workplace could be assets in parenting special children. As first noted in Chapter 2, it will be worth your while to sit down with someone and, with an open mind, list the things we traditionally think of as assets. Then list those things people tend to think of as liabilities. Brainstorm with one or more persons you know well and trust, then imagine using these qualities to help raise a special child. You may decide you want to try parenting children who are very different from those you had first imagined. Talk with your licensing worker about this and get his/her input. And don't be afraid to "take the plunge"! People like you are greatly needed.

Examples of qualities — for better or worse	Type of child who could benefit from them
Controlling	Delinquent, group home
Nurturing	Needy
Easygoing	Independent
New foster parent (very invested and conscientious)	High-needs child
Like to teach	High academic needs
Friendly, accepting, supportive, self-assured	Work with child's family
Your own qualities	**Type of child or needs**

In the next two chapters we take a closer look at these issues, including what is in the best interests of the *child.*

CHAPTER 5

Matching You with Types of Children

It is the job of the licensing worker to match foster and adoptive parents with a child or children who will do well in their home. *It is __not__ the job of the foster care worker to find a child who will please __you__.* Please reread the previous sentence! *The licensing worker has the best interests of __the child__ in mind.* With adoption, of course, there's more emphasis on the adopting family's needs, and with guardianships or other voluntary parenting situations, only you need to decide which children to take in.

But in foster care, children come into the system with certain needs and requirements, and placements are made to accommodate those needs, first and foremost. You will always have the choice of which children to accept or not accept, but you were probably chosen more for your skills than your desires.

Often parents enter the foster care or adoption system with the idea of taking a beautiful little baby, raising it to adulthood, and living "happily ever after." However, beautiful, healthy, easy-to-raise babies come along only about once every 10 years for a waiting couple. If you want to foster or adopt *now,* you will need to consider an older child, a sibling group, a medically or mentally handicapped child, a biracial child, or even a child from another country. Foster care agencies have a tremendous need for homes for these "other" children. Homes for teens are probably the most difficult to find. What parent wants to take on a child who is rude, self-centered, behind in school, and oppositional — and, oh yes, has purple hair?! Well, believe it or not, there are a few such parents, but the agencies are begging for more.

There's a pitfall many of us fall into when we enter the foster care system. We're so anxious to help all those "poor" children, we take on too much. It's far better to start small and modestly, then graduate to a group home later. Parents with wisdom and patience know this, of course, but I didn't. I was just lucky to have a wise worker!

All my life, I imagined a group home with 12 (yes, 12!) kids, a big old farmhouse, a barn full of ponies for the kids, and evenings in front of a roaring fire, playing games, or doing homework with them. *Cut!* Reality check.

When my husband and I first became licensed foster parents, we got a teenage boy, blind and disturbed, from a terribly abusive home. We kept asking the licensing worker when we would receive our next placement. She would just smile and tell us we had to wait until the right child came along. What we didn't know was that she had placed a very high-needs child with new and enthusiastic foster parents, who in turn would put a lot of time and energy into him. She didn't want to jeopardize a stable placement by adding a second child! She would occasionally increase our daily stipend according to criteria we didn't even know about. Admittedly, the extra money helped, but we were totally in the dark about her reasons. She knew that if she told us her thinking, we would have objected, saying we could handle another child. I now know that the boy was the highest-need child I ever parented, and adding a second would have been a mistake.

Of course, 20 years ago the system was far different from today. Placements were expected to last for years in many cases, and stability was difficult to achieve with severely needy children. Caseworkers also had much more discretion in the area of daily rates and services offered than they do now. It is the era of "managed care" and "documentation." Our state has a point system to determine the rate of board and care, and budgets are carefully monitored. Responsibility for services is shuffled around among agencies, with no one wanting to foot the bill. Thus, it's important for foster parents to educate themselves educate themselves and learn how to deal with the maze of agencies and service providers they will need.

Children also tend to be more difficult today. Oh, I know, you'll say I sound like the person who had to "walk 10 miles to school in a blizzard, uphill both ways"! But it's well-documented that things are different now. Placements are made on the basis of a point system (severely violent delinquents get the most points). Payments are made on a point system (the more time and service you give your child, the higher the daily rate). Nowadays, courts typically send children back home after shorter time periods in foster care. In addition, some states are demanding faster permanency plans for children, and foster parents are adopting more than they did in the past. This reduces the number of available foster homes. The resulting domino effect is that new homes must constantly be licensed, and experienced foster parents are becoming more rare.

Another difficulty that requires your education is the turnover rate in foster care workers. Statistics in Michigan, for example, show that social workers consider work in foster care "entry level," and the average rate of turnover among such staff people is only *one year*. What this means is that, in a very short time, you likely will know more about fostering than your caseworker. Licensing workers often are much more knowledgeable than the workers overseeing the placements, and it would behoove you to get to know the licensing workers well, so that appropriate placements are made in your home.

I found that learning the rules and regulations of the system — and what services are available to my children — has helped me a great deal in advocating for them. An important way to do this is to attend support group meetings. Almost all agencies have them. Other foster parents will be your greatest assets. In fact, many agencies are using mentoring systems, linking experienced parents with newly licensed parents, in order to ease the load of the overworked social workers, as well as help the foster parents feel at ease when asking questions.

So, when I list my assets, I include extensive knowledge of the foster and adoptive systems. The years I spent as a foster parent and foster care worker helped me become an advocate for other foster parents in our area. I learned how to "work the system" — for me, my husband, *and* the parents I was advocating for as a friend and caseworker. That way I was able to get better resources for my own foster kids, as well as the foster children under my general jurisdiction. I don't know of many social workers who would object to sharing pages of their manuals with you or teaching you about their job requirements. The more you know, the easier you can make their job and yours.

Perhaps you're wondering what *specific types of factors* the licensing worker is considering in order to place children. Following is a partial list. The most important criterion is clearly stated in the law — and that is always to do what is in *"the best interests of the child."* If you hear workers or judges speaking of the "best-interest criterion," this is what they mean. It's possible to overlook some other needs or justify unusual circumstances and services if they meet the "best-interest criterion." After reading the list, see if you can think of other elements to add.

- Possible placement with someone with existing relationship with the child, such as a relative or surrogate/mentor.[1]
- Least restrictive placement in light of the conditions.[2]
- Possible placement with siblings.
- Similar ethnic or social background of family.
- Proximity to the child's bio-family.
- Proximity to the child's school district — or similarity of school districts if child is required to transfer.
- Proximity to child's need for special services.
- Same or similar religious orientation, if this is an issue with the child's family.
- Foster family's willingness or ability to continue placement in the future, if determined to be in the child's best interests by the court.
- _____

---

[1] Relatives are always considered first. Think of that when you want a "cute little 3-year-old." Why didn't the family want him/her? What's wrong with this child?

[2] The court wishes to place children in the community, not in institutions. Thus they look for the least restrictive and most home-like placement possible, and they don't increase restrictions without a court hearing and good reason. In addition, increased restrictions cost more money, so they must be justified.

CHAPTER 6

Using Strengths, Dealing with Weaknesses, in the Daily Struggle

A cynic (but a realist) once said, "The devil is in the details." Raising children is a daily struggle, and it's the daily details that can cause most of the problems. Some people are able to deal with a major crisis from time to time, but they get worn down when it comes to getting up on time each day, maintaining the consistency that children need, and following through on behavior plans. Therefore, it's in the everyday grind of life that your strengths come into play — and where you'll learn to compensate for your weaknesses.

* * *

As touched on in Chapter 2 and elaborated on in Chapter 4, brainstorm with someone else. Be creative in coming up with a system that enhances your abilities. And don't get discouraged as you work out the kinks in your system. It can take a long time to get it right, but it's well worth it.

I have ADHD. This means I have difficulty remembering things, being consistent, and following through. I become scattered and disorganized very easily. Children with ADHD usually have a mom to keep them on track, but I don't, and there are so many things going on in my large family that it could easily deteriorate into chaos. Over the years, therefore, I developed a system that worked for both my foster kids and me. It involves a lot of paperwork, but parts of it could be useful and adaptable for your situation, so I'll describe it.

I sat down and listed the expectations I had for my children's daily routine. This included a detailed morning schedule, which helped keep them on time in the mornings, along with reminders posted at strategic locations throughout the house. The big advantage of having it all in writing is that the foster children coming into the home have it in front of them too, and it's quickly clear to them what's expected of them. But most of my foster children weren't oriented to the written instructions and literal methods I was using, so I needed to adapt and teach.

Never put a long and detailed list on a wall for a child! And understand that all of us become used to the things around us and don't see them after several days or weeks. Because of this, I frequently change the signs. Adding humor helps, as do a variety of colors, type styles, pictures, and so on. For example, here's the sign taped on the bathroom wall, next to the medicine cabinet:

Morning schedule
6:00 — Get up and dress
6:15 — Barn
6:30 — Kitchen
7:00 — Brush teeth, gather coats and books
7:15 — Bus stop

This leaves no doubt about when and where a child must be in the morning. It also trains even young children to get on a schedule and keep moving, so they're on time for the bus.

How would you adapt it for elementary kids? With pictures of clocks, as well as pictures *they* cut out of magazines or draw, telling them what to do at what time. I would draw a clock with hands set at 6 o'clock and a stick figure sitting up in bed or dressing. Then I'd add a clock with hands at 6:15, with a stick figure feeding the dog.

I wouldn't put in many details, but instead I'd put up a sign in their room with the three things to do between 6 and 6:30 and a sign in the kitchen that shows a place setting — including bowl, spoon, glass, and napkin. Even a 2-year-old can be trained to take the bowl and spoon to the sink after eating.

In the bathroom, it would work well to place a picture of a child brushing his/her teeth, cut out of a magazine, and, after it, pictures of a backpack and coat (to remind children that teeth brushing is the last thing before heading out the door).

Lots of details? Yes, but these are the things this system can teach: setting the alarm and getting yourself up, staying on schedule, being organized, remembering responsibilities (the dog), healthy life habits, learning to tell time, and reading improvement.

But, you ask, how does this relate to *my* strengths and weaknesses? To begin with, I have thought out what I expect from my children, and I won't keep changing the plan and confusing them. Second, I transfer the schedule to their daily chart, which is posted on the fridge, and how well they follow their schedule affects their allowance and reward system. When I check the chart, it allows me to see at a glance whether or not they're on track and to determine who deserves a large allowance and who does not.

> **❗ Don't feel sorry for them!**

The next page shows a detailed chart and a smaller and simpler chart for young children. Before I began using a written system, I couldn't remember who did what, and my own follow-through was terrible. The chart was developed for my group home when I had to keep track of eight children at once, and it worked well for me. It also provided a visible record for the children, their parents, and the caseworker. The records were put into a loose-leaf notebook and saved for a few months. If there was something notable on the chart, I could put it into the individual's file, indicating to the caseworker how the child compared with others. On occasion, I also shared it with the child's therapist. Did the child get everything checked, doing his/her best to follow the rules and behave? Did the child slack off, cheat, and fail to complete chores? These things can be useful to know and report, as well as giving you items to work on with the child.

You can use signs for the dinner hour, dividing chores and responsibilities, or put up reminders of bedtime routines and bedtimes too. For example — again, for the teenage foster children — I had a list of bedtimes posted in the hallway by the bedrooms. This eliminated all arguments over bedtimes and made everything clear to everyone.

Bedtimes
Ages 0-12, 8:30
13-14, 9:00
15-16, 9:30
17-18, 10:00
Half-hour later on weekends and holidays

Using different colors of paper, highlighting with color, adding pictures, and putting a joke or saying on the sign help get the children to notice. Or have all of them read and initial it, proving they were told and shown.

Chore chart

WEEK OF 3/29/02	John								Susan								Aaron								Jane							
Up at 6:00																																
Make Bed & Clean Rm.																																
Chores																																
Help w/ Breakfast																																
A.M. Attitude																																
Dishes/ Pills																																
Brush Teeth																																
Home-work																																
P.M. Attitude																																
Exercise/ Fresh Air																																
Yard Work																																
In Room on Time																																
Lights Out																																
Assigned Room*	Living Room								Basement								Upstairs Bathroom								Study							
Care for:**	Sonny, King, Barn floor (loose hay)								Water all horses, Strings on ground								August, Mighty, Puppies								Gunner, Trigger, Rabbit							
Bonus/ Penalty																																
Total																																

* Each child is assigned a room to keep clean for the week.

** Each child has the responsibility of a horse, a dog, and one farm item. Being responsible for animals is, in some ways, like caring for a child. Children and animals must be taken care of whether the owners are tired, gone, or have other problems. They must hire a "sitter" when gone. Children may pay each other *only occasionally* to take over their assigned responsibilities.

For young children simple charts, with pictures instead of words, are effective. The parent, of course, goes over the chart *with* the child on at least a daily basis. Rewards should be more immediate for younger children; these can be pennies in a jar, poker chips, stars, or other tangible things the child can count.

Amelia's chores

JOB	MON	TUE	WED	THU	FRI	SAT	
							Get up on time
							Make bed
							Put clothes in hamper
							Set table
							Feed dog
							Turn off light

! If you promise a reward -- give it!

At the end of the week, a previously determined special reward is given, according to points earned. For example: 10 points = go out for ice cream with Mom or Dad; 15 points = rent a movie and make popcorn, then watch as a family; 20 points = a matchbox car; and so on.

An example of another kind of chart is shown next. This is a tool that foster parents would probably use more than parents who have the same children in their home all the time. It can be very difficult for foster children to know all the rules of a home, and they often ask other children in the home, which is a bad idea. Another child will slant things, leave things out, and editorialize (tell the new child if a parent enforces, how to get out of things, and other "tips"). The chart makes things clear for everyone, including caseworkers and parents.

Sometimes I take a chart into school for individual education planning conferences (IEPCs), and the special education teacher can then bridge between school and home, thereby reinforcing the expectations at home. Although some may think this is too much written material, I have found it's a great teaching tool for kids who always have had to operate orally in their own home. They begin learning to read signs, follow directions, and check all the details on the page. Another learning tool!

Expectations

Daily	Weekly
Bedroom	Thorough cleaning
Assigned room	Thorough cleaning
Feed/water animal	Groom animal
1 hour of brain work	Cook 1 meal
½ hour of exercise	Laundry
½ hour of outside work	1 hour for family project

Additional mental models for encouraging children in their progress can be found in Appendix E.

More on strengths and weaknesses

The previous discussion offers a sample, detailed method to get you thinking about your own system. Suppose you're a person who is easygoing and laid-back about housework, but you know you have to motivate yourself and the family to get going and put some structure into domestic duties. Maybe you can sit down together and get the family to suggest ways to do this without getting obsessive about charts and paperwork. The children placed in your home may be the older children who have taken care of themselves for years because of dysfunctional parents, and they likely will do better without pressure.

What if you're nitpicky and a "neat freak"? You may get children in your home who are slobs. What can you do? The choices are:

- Ignore the mess.
- Clean it up yourself.
- Set up a behavior-modification plan for the child. (You may even involve the therapist or caseworker in the setup.)

And your attention to structure and detail might be just what the child in your home needed to get his/her life back under control.

Suppose you're an extra nurturing type of person, and your home is about lots of hugs, praise, and warm cookies from the oven? A needy and deprived child will soak up the warmth, but all that might drive another kind of person crazy!

Are you controlling? Well, if you're not, you might be surprised how a controlling foster parent actually deals with situations! Here's a typical scenario involving foster parents in *a group home for delinquent teenagers* (not in all foster parenting situations):

Dinah asks her foster mother if she may go to the football game and dance on Friday night at school. Mom asks:

"How will you get there?

"Who else is going?

"What time does it start and end?

"Who is chaperoning?

"How much does it cost? Do you have enough saved from allowance?

"Did you bring home your grade slip, signed by all your teachers?

"How will you get home?"

Dinah gives all the appropriate responses, knowing that she will be driven and picked up by the foster parents, not another teen. But the parents don't stop there. They call during the week and check the agenda with the school. They ask who is chaperoning the dance. They ask how closely the students are observed in the stands. *Then* they give Dinah permission to go.

Does it end there? *No!* Mom drives Dinah and any other kids who need a ride. She makes sure they're dressed appropriately, decently, and don't have outrageous makeup on. She drops them off. Before she leaves, she watches them pay and go in.

An hour later, around halftime, *Mom returns to the game.* (She is known by the staff — and allowed in — to check on her kids.) She first looks for them, to be sure they haven't gone off with their friends to drink, smoke, or who-knows-what? Then she goes up to them and says hi. Why? So they know she *does* check on them. In addition, she'll occasionally say goodbye, then return immediately. She has learned that they expect to see her only once during the evening, and she has had to deal with kids who took off immediately after her departure. This controlling Mom tries to stay one step ahead of the kids!

Next she checks in with another parent who also has been observing the kids from the stands. *Three foster parents have networked* and have set up a system so that only one of them has to attend the game, giving the others a break.

After returning home this time, Mom settles down in front of the TV. But here's where the teamwork goes into action! The kids know that their foster father will be picking them up from the dance. What they *don't* know is that he has planned to come an hour early to check into their dress and behavior inside the school! If he finds that they have changed clothing, are not in the building, or are behaving inappropriately, there will be consequences. Parents and teens have discussed the types of consequences for such behaviors, but they don't expect him this particular night. After checking in, Dad goes out to the car to take a nap. He then drives them home, and everyone goes to bed.

If all that seems like it would take a great deal of energy, it does! But the kind of foster child placed in that group home is *a high-needs child who was placed there because the parents can follow through with this kind of plan.* They are probably also paid a higher daily rate than the average foster parents. Maybe some children would go crazy under a system like this, but there are many who need it. The controlling nature of these parents might be a serious liability in the workplace or most social settings, but such individuals are ideal for running a group foster home!

You'll be required to keep *records and files* on any foster children you take, and a good therapist may require behavior logs or other paperwork from you for the child's behavior plan. But all kinds of people keep all kinds of files, and only a very few are unable to comply with the regulations. Obsessive-compulsive people can provide detailed weekly reports, monthly reports, medical records, and even reports of a child's activities down to the quarter hour! More easygoing and non-clerical types just throw all the related stuff into a file on the child, and let it go at that. Most of us fall somewhere in between. But I have learned from being a case manager that all kinds are needed in the world of foster care, for there are all kinds of kids and all kinds of needs. The placement agency would fail miserably if it just had one kind of home to offer a child.

One more example may be helpful for social workers and foster parents, as well as for adoptive and biological parents of medically fragile children.

I once was called in as a contract worker in an agency that had no foster care worker and was having trouble filling the position. The foster care cases were in shambles, and the foster parents had had no support for several months. There had been an unusually large turnover in the position, and two of the recent workers had been brand-new, so they knew little about the job. What a challenge! As I worked through each case, pulled the information together, and met the individuals involved, I put my creative instincts to work. I helped the foster parents develop behavior plans, implement the workers' case plans, and write the reports for the courts. One case, in particular, intrigued me.

A baby who was born brain-damaged and with extreme physical needs was placed in one of our foster homes. The child had not been expected to live, but since being placed in foster care had begun to thrive. The family was a highly devout Christian family; they believed that God had sent this child to them. They were devoting their entire life to her care. Their children were home-schooled and assisted in some ways, and the parents took turns sleeping in two-hour shifts at night. The girl had been in their home for several months, and there was an upcoming trial to remove the rights of the child's parents, giving the foster parents the opportunity to adopt. I visited the home, met the child, and renewed my acquaintance with the foster parents who had attended my pre-service classes prior to being licensed. They asked me for a couple of things the child needed, and I cheerfully told them I'd get to work on it right away.

When I returned to the office, I was appalled to learn that these parents were receiving just $18 a day to care for their foster child. If the same child were in a hospital or institution, it would be costing the state more than $200 per day, with the fees of specialists added on top of that! I knew that once they adopted the child, the adoption subsidy would be set and could not be raised without great difficulty. I was determined to do something about it. My first call was to a foster care supervisor, to ask what the maximum daily rate was and how to get it for them. He told me documentation was the key, and the top rate could be as high as $80, but it took approval up the line (from supervisors, district heads, and others). I knew the foster mother was incredibly detail-oriented and obsessive about recordkeeping, so at least on one level this would be a snap. However, by the time she and I had finished our work, we had done enough research and writing to produce a masters' thesis!

This is not the place to give you all the details. But here's a quick overview. The foster mother provided a daily routine broken into 15-minute blocks, I provided research detailing the cost of hiring specialists to do all the things the parents did for the child, and much more. She listed the number of specialists the child was taken to each week, month, and quarter, along with the number of miles to get there.

She listed the medications and doses. She counted diapers and the number of times she spent cleaning the child's feeding tubes. It went on and on.

The supervisor then requested a list of anything that was *currently* being provided from other agencies, such as the Red Cross, school, Goodwill, and so on. We had to access more helping agencies, such as community mental health, to provide some respite periods. She provided reports from every doctor, the special education file, the court, and my reports. We had a report that was now an inch thick, and had taken months to compile. Our report justified a daily rate of $96 a day, which I requested. I knew the ceiling, but I also knew that the decision-making personnel would attempt to lower it, cut the budget, and find other ways to provide care, so I allowed for cuts.

The court terminated parental rights, adoption proceedings began, and we received approval for $80 per day for the adopting parents! Thus, obsessive recordkeeping, total immersion in infant care, and what some might consider extreme religious views all had their place in this child's life.

If this child had had a parent who didn't keep good records, we would never have succeeded. So, as you can see, it takes all kinds, and you have a place in the system and in the life of a child … somewhere. Don't give up!

For those of you who are parenting grandchildren, adopted children, neighbor children, or others who aren't foster children, some of the material in this book will be helpful, and some will be less so. But keep reading!

CHAPTER 7

The Resiliency of a Child

I have heard it said that children survive in spite of their parents. At times I know this is true! For I have made many mistakes and you will too. But your children will probably survive, grow up, and become fully functioning adults. The key is to help them become productive, interactive, happy adults as well. They must be able to interact appropriately in the world around them, with the people around them. They must be able to connect with others, both on the surface and intimately. And many of us hope our children also will produce grandchildren for us to enjoy as we move on beyond our own child-rearing years.

* * *

It's no secret that children tend to be more resilient than adults. The phrase "set in his ways" describes older adults. Terms for younger people are words and phrases like "impressionable" and "flexible" and "eager to learn." We study the changing phases of children's growth and development, along with the influences on their personality and behavior. We talk about them in terms like "sponges that soak up knowledge." But they also must be resilient to withstand life's tough circumstances, losses, crises, and pain. And with children's lack of power and control over their life, they may have to deal with even more of these than their parents.

The child you are raising, who isn't yours by birth, already has suffered multiple losses. He/she may have suffered birth trauma, physical deformity or handicap, neglect, or abuse. Such children may have had to adjust to several homes, caregivers, personalities, and demands. They may have even had to move into a totally different culture, including language, customs, and habits. Yet the children are still able to smile, to grow, to play, and to learn! And, in most cases, your child can love. We can only imagine our own response to being "placed in foster care," or removed from all we had ever known of life, and given to someone else to "control." For these things are unlikely to happen to any adults in their lifetime, unless they become a refugee. Yes, your child can bounce back and adjust to life with you, growing more and more "normal" each day.

If you are a foster or adoptive parent, you may receive a child or children who have acted out of their anger and pain to the degree that they come under control of the courts as delinquents. Know that beneath the defiance, behind the bravado, besides the rudeness, are a heart and soul and pain. Social workers often say that a child who enters the foster care system as a delinquent is just an abuse/neglect case who started falling through the cracks. You may feel that statement places unfair blame on the parents, but social workers have seen it happen over and over again.

A crisis occurs. The police are called. A girl is apprehended for shoplifting in a department store. After doing their investigation, the authorities uncover a multitude of problems in her home and ask themselves whether, underneath it all, she was attempting to get someone to notice her by her illegal act. This is sometimes termed "a cry for help."

A fight breaks out between a boy and his stepfather, and he is told to "hit the road." The teen enters the "runaway" system and begins to commit crimes to obtain basic necessities. When he's finally picked up by police, and an investigation ensues, the authorities learn some new facts. His father and mother divorced because of Dad's alcoholism, and the boy has been watching over his younger sisters the past 10 years. His mother had to choose between her new husband and the son who defies him. She either gives up her security and income to defend him, or she stands by his stepfather's decision to force him out of the home.

She reasons that he is 16 years old and probably will leave in the next year or two anyway. But she has the rest of her life to live, two more children to finish raising, and the bills to pay.

These delinquent teens still may turn their life around and grow up to become happy and healthy adults — if they're given the tools to do so.

Then there are the children who are born with countless physical and/or mental problems. The foster parents who take in "medically fragile" children often have to face the fact that the children they hold in their arms and hearts may not live longer than a few months or years. Or they may have to accept that their child will never be able to care for himself/herself because of mental or physical handicaps that make it impossible.

Of course, many young children enter the system as "neglect wards." These are children who have been experiencing pain and loss in large doses for several years. This is because someone must first learn of the abuse and prompt an investigation, and the courts must then give the parents time to change things. If, after trying every possible kind of intervention, the parents still can't (or won't) raise their child appropriately, parental rights can be terminated, and the child is put up for adoption or placed in foster care. Some of these children's stories are incredibly painful. Adults are able to inflict horrendous amounts of suffering on these small people. The "creativity" of abusive parents/adults is unbelievable!

Of course, some parents don't *willfully* neglect their children. As Dr. Ruby Payne points out in her analysis of class issues in the United States, these adults are merely repeating a multi-generational cycle in which *they* grew up. They know no other way. But that doesn't change the way the children suffer pain and loss. Yet, somehow, many of these resilient young people still sing and dance and brighten the lives of those of us who are raising them!

Perhaps only God can answer the question of how children survive what adults do to them. But if we learn how children think, understand how they act out, and give them our best, we can certainly increase the chances that they will, indeed, survive.

Survival skills

What are some of the things that we can give our children to help them survive in the "real world"? Some of us call them "survival tools." Others formally name them "Skills for Independent Living." Dr. Payne calls them resources. Once again, the parent (you) must be creative in figuring out just what your own children need, based upon your assessment of them. *But always remember that you are putting your own values and expectations into the assessment, and you could be totally wrong!*

Perhaps you feel that "success" is being productive and contributing something worthwhile to society. Or maybe you believe that the ability to merely stay alive is a "success." The important thing is to try to predict the environment your children will have to survive in and build on the strengths and assets they already have. If you're a middle-class suburbanite and take in foster children from the inner city, they will have a set of needs that are much different from your own children.

If, on the other hand, you live in a downtown high rise and the children will be moving to a farm when they're released from your custody, they won't need to know things to help them survive in the downtown area. They'll need to learn to pound a nail, dig a hole, muck a stall, milk a cow, and gather the eggs! These scenes may seem to be an exaggeration, but they are laid out to point out the need for assessment, as well as *your ability to truly understand your child.*

Many city kids came to live with us on our farm. Part of my success as a foster parent resulted from my ability to gain immediate respect from them by doing tasks well that they had never seen done before. Correspondingly, part of *their* new self-respect stemmed from their pride in learning to do these new tasks well. But no matter how well they adapted or how conscientiously they learned, none of these skills had direct correlation to their survival in the inner-city environment when they left our home.

Another parent/trainer told the following story. A foster mother came to her caseworker and cried because the judge had sent her young foster children home to a mother she believed was very neglectful and had not changed. The foster mother felt the judge did not understand the gravity of the situation and the danger of neglect the children were in. The girls had been half-starved when she first got them and had put on a lot of weight and become much healthier in her care.

The trainer asked why they were malnourished in the first place. The foster mother told her the mom was on drugs and sometimes did not wake up to feed them meals. The girls were 4 and 6, and thus they couldn't cook for themselves. What survival skills would such youngsters need?

A few weeks later the girls were taken out of their home again and placed back with the same foster mother. This time she was prepared! She taught them how to put a chair up to the cupboard and climb to reach the peanut butter. She taught them how to put it on the bread. They learned how to open a hot dog package and get out a hot dog, then put it in the microwave and set it for one minute. She taught them to handle the hot dog when it was hot, so they wouldn't get burned, and she helped the 6-year-old practice pouring milk and juice into a cup.

Then she enlisted the caseworker (teamwork) to follow through in their home, showing the girls how to work their own microwave, and asking their mother to keep foods in the house they now knew how to work with (involving the parent in the treatment plan). The mother was cooperative because she didn't want to lose her daughters again. The final piece of information the foster mother gave the girls was teaching them how and when to call 9-1-1.

When the judge returned the girls to their mother the next time, the foster mother was confident that she had given them survival tools they would use for the rest of their life.

It's true that children are highly resilient creatures, but the more survival tools and resources we can give them the better.

In addition to learning how to obtain and prepare food, survival tools can be many different things. You might teach a sexually abused child how to repel advances and report them. You might teach a teenager a number of things about the adult world they'll soon be entering. You might show children how to set the alarm clock and get dressed by themselves.

For many foster parents, knowing that you have given these children the gift of survival has eased the pain of losing them. Over the years I have often been surprised to hear what children learned from me or took from my house that helped them later. That feels good!

It's obvious, of course, that teenagers need to know adult skills for survival in the adult world. Other places in this book speak to this in more detail. With teens, motivation is a key factor. In addition, there are many skills they'll need that don't come immediately to mind. I worked in one home years ago where there were three teens and two adults. All five of these people were using an outhouse, while a perfectly good toilet went unused in the bathroom. Why? *The toilet was running and no one knew how to fix it, so they turned the water off instead!* These people were amazed when I went in, opened the toilet top, and untangled the chain, allowing the plug to work properly! Can your teens change a light bulb? Pound a nail? Turn off gas or water in an emergency? Unplug a drain? Change the oil in the car? Empty the vacuum bag? You get the idea, I'm sure. The kids can learn these things and save themselves a great deal of money, discomfort, and problems in the future. In fact, learning such skills will give them self-esteem and win admiration from their friends and families.

You are living with these children during their so-called "formative years." The things you teach them now will increase their resiliency, strengthen their resources, and enhance their ability to survive in what can be a very tough world.

CHAPTER 8

Expectations and Reality

Should this chapter include the parent's expectations of the parenting experience? Or should we discuss the expectations of a child who comes into your life and has dreamed of belonging to a family for so long? Perhaps the discussion should include the foster parents' expectations of what kinds of children are going to be placed with them — and what the system will be doing to help them.

No experience in life is exactly as we expected it to be. Think about your dreams of growing up and "doing whatever you wanted to do." Think about your idealization of the marriage experience. Think about children you may have already raised — and the surprises that came your way through that experience. The list goes on and on: job, divorce, death of a loved one, your infallibility, your immortality (dreams of a teenage mind!), and how big your savings account would be by this time! Parenting other people's children is no different. The expectations and the reality are often very far apart. But let's look at the expectations of parents compared with those of the children in their care.

Your view vs. Their view

Your view	Their view
Marriage	Loyalty
Discipline	Rules
Money	Clothing
Authority	Love
Respect	Time
Laws	Possessions
Goals	Family

Discuss any one of the above topics with any child you meet and you'll be amazed at their world-view. So, begin by knowing that, by and large, they aren't on the same page you're on!

Again, we turn to the work of Dr. Ruby Payne. Her studies of class values and lifestyles impact this aspect of child rearing to such an extent that they can make for success or failure in the entire process.

The expectations parents have for their children vary with the parents' own socioeconomic background:

- Wealthy parents usually expect their children to become professionals and have positions of power and wealth. Well-to-do parents often manipulate their children's social life, contacts, and even their marriages (yes, plural!).

- Middle-class parents often expect their children to have gainful employment, an education beyond high school, and a comfortable lifestyle with a family — that is, after marrying the person of their choice (as long as he/she is of similar background).

- The parents of a child from multi-generational poverty may not even be looking that far into the future but, if pressed, may tell you they expect their child to get a job and stay out of jail.

So, if wealthy and middle-class foster parents receive into their home children from a background of poverty, how will their expectations differ? Or, if a child from a background of wealth or middle-class parents is placed in a foster care situation with parents in poverty, how well will they fit in? And how will the other children in the home get along with the newcomer?

If your expectations for this child are unrealistic, you will not help him/her succeed. If your expectations are the same for your bio-child and the adopted or fostered child, who has experienced severe trauma and delays, you will be sadly disappointed. In my opinion, that is why relatively few rich people foster. Many of the behavioral expectations in wealth are hard for a child from poverty to live up to. Thus, the child would be frustrated and the adult angry. The value system tends to be foreign to the child. For example:

Mrs. Wealthy is having her husband's CEO and the local candidate for governor to her home for dinner. As her foster child has now reached 17, she feels he should become familiar with local politics and learn to discuss important topics with dinner guests. Tommy Foster Child doesn't want to discuss important topics, doesn't want to wear a suit to dinner, and could care less about either of the guests. Thus, his attitude is sullen, his table manners horrible, and his conversation filled with "street talk" and poor grammar in front of the guests. Mrs. Wealthy is horrified and wants to punish the child. She may even call the caseworker to have him moved as soon as possible.

Or take another example from the upper class:

Mrs. Culture is talking with her friends. She is quite upset after a weekend trip to Chicago with her two teenage foster boys. Her conversation goes something like:

"Well, I have never seen such ungrateful children in my life! My husband and I arranged a fantastic weekend for them, and they acted as though they were bored to death. First, we explored the Historical Museum, then the Museum of Science and Industry. We took them to a symphony and to the finest steakhouse in Chicago. They had the nerve to run ahead in the museums, buy soda, and hang around the entrance. At the symphony, they talked constantly, even to the point of others having to get up and move. And you should have seen them at the steakhouse! A hundred dollars a plate, and they wolfed the food down like a pack of hungry animals! When they drank, they dribbled ice water down their face, and they used the seafood fork to eat the prime rib and steak. All weekend all they wanted to do was go back to the hotel and watch Pay-TV in the room. I wonder why we even try to expose them to culture. They don't appreciate anything we do!"

What would you tell this foster mother? What are your thoughts on the situation? Would *you* like to live in this foster home? Think about the expectations of the parents. Can the kids ever live up to them? Think about what kind of expectations the kids would have about a trip to Chicago. Can you see why they were unhappy?

One way to avoid the type of situation we describe here is to carefully assess your own expectations, discuss them with your foster/adoptive home licenser, and with some experienced foster parents. If your expectations are pretty far from what the licenser calls reality, should you still go ahead and foster? Probably. But you may have to adjust your thinking and clarify with your licenser what your intentions are — in order to avoid "a trip to Chicago." Either the licenser will have to place only certain types of kids with you (who are very few in number), or you will have to alter your expectations and discuss events and trips with the children ahead of time. You can listen to their ideas, think about their expectations compared with your own, and perhaps change some of the agenda. (Also going to an arcade or spending time at the beach might help balance out the trip. Get their input.) If you're going to request certain behaviors ahead of time, perhaps you can work out some compromises. *Communicate* with them! Find out what they want to get out of the trip and try to work in some things that they'll clearly have fun doing. Become a dictator, deaf to their desires, and you can plan on having a miserable trip!

In this example, it's easy to see how mutual understanding of values is essential. It will be important for you to learn what kind of lifestyle the children have had before you can effectively <u>motivate</u> them, parent them, or succeed with them. It also will be necessary for you to be open with them about <u>your expectations</u> — and realistic about their ability to meet them.

If a child from an extremely different background from yours comes to your home, many direct discussions will be needed during the course of daily activities. Standards and values should be discussed, *compromises and flexibility should be taught*. You will need a clear understanding of the difference between disobedient behavior, oppositional behavior, and behavior caused by lack of understanding or ability. During your discussions, make it clear to the child that there aren't "bad" or "good" differences in style or values, only that you are offering choices.

A huge mistake that parents make is not interacting with the children who visit their home — *and* not observing their children's interactions. Parents not only should watch young children (teaching them to share, build things, be creative, and work out problems peacefully), but also observe what's really going on with teens.

The therapist who worked with our foster children did a session with the early adolescent child *and* the parent that he called "Sex Ed 101." During this session, expectations were discussed, and rules of dating were laid out.

You don't need a therapist to do it. Here's a sample of how it might go:

Parent: "When you reach puberty, hormones begin moving through your body, and you may have new feelings about the opposite sex. In other words, boys are no longer 'geeks,' and girls no longer have 'cooties.' Have you ever felt these things?"

Lisa: "Well, not yet, I guess."

Parent: "Well, there are things about smell, staying clean, having periods, and suddenly noticing every little thing about your body. You may feel like you aren't as pretty as the other girls in school, or you may worry for days about a zit on your face. Know what? So does everyone else!"

This is not a big lecture, and it should be interactive, with children and parents all taking part. There's no necessity to discuss sexually transmitted diseases or sexual acts at this point.

The parents then check with the kids and determine if they heard and understood what was discussed. When everyone is comfortable, they continue.

Parents ask children for their observations about couples touching, kissing in public, and "sex talk" they have heard — and whether they think it was appropriate. Each person in the room discusses his/her own feelings about these things.

Even if children are giving appropriate responses, it's helpful for parents to talk openly about their views and clarify their expectations in the area of sex and interaction. No approach is foolproof, of course, but candid, caring conversations between parent and child go a long way toward improving the odds for success.

Rules regarding these expectations are recommended. They should be made clear, and the consequences for breaking them need to be discussed. You could say something like this: "You must show us appropriate behavior before you'll be allowed to date. There are certain things little kids can do — like sitting on someone's lap — that teens may not. And there are behaviors that are considered bad manners or inappropriate for both adolescents and adults. In addition, because of natural and normal human desires, you shouldn't put yourself in a position where you might give in to temptation and be sorry later. Basically, this is what we expect of all our children, regardless of age."

Then, so there's no confusion, you might want to go over your expectations both orally and on a written list. Encourage your children to ask why if they don't understand a rule — or discuss specific situations with you.

Our own expectations are listed here as a guide, but appropriate behaviors vary in homes, cultures, neighborhoods, and parts of the country, so list *your own.*

- No guests are to be in bedrooms.
- No one is to be lying down *with another person* for any reason, including watching TV.
- No "head in lap" positions, or sitting between each others' knees.
- No sitting on someone else's lap.
- No tickling, wrestling, or other "contact" activities.
- No "making out" or "parking"; handholding is OK.
- Know the differences in kissing. A "peck" of affection is far different from a "French" (or tongue) kiss. One is OK, one is *not.*
- Keep moving! Stay active and around other people; interact with the family.
- Plan your activities; down time is dangerous time.
- Call us for a ride, no questions asked, if you're in a bad spot.

- No drugs or alcohol — ever — but the effects of one or both in connection with a dating relationship can be especially devastating.
- When in doubt, ask yourself this: If one or both of your parents were sitting next to you, would you be doing this?
- Respect yourself and each other. Keep things at a "surface" level, not a "deep" one.

Parents will then move on to very specific guidelines of what they expect from their children when interacting, "going with," dating, or associating with the opposite sex. Asking pointed questions would be one way to do this. An example might be:

"Judy, if you're going with a boy, is it OK to hold hands at school?"

Or "Jay, should you feel free to put your hand on a girl's leg, if she is your 'girlfriend'?"

After they answer the specific questions, you should be clear about your expectations of them. You might want to say something like this:

"We expect our children to always respect themselves and others. We don't think it's appropriate to touch and feel each other in private places before marriage. If a couple is dating, they should be with groups of young people or their families for several months, not alone in the back seats of cars or kissing in corners and dark places."

Be careful not to phrase this in language the child doesn't understand, to act superior, or to talk down to them. If your child's vocabulary is limited, use words he/she understands. Make it serious enough, but friendly and comfortable, and pay attention both to their answers *and* body language.

Parents should always be sure to check with the children about what they hear from these discussions and not give long lectures. Other times should be made for further discussion too. A good time to stop is when the child begins to fidget or have trouble paying attention.

Good times to talk with kids are when you're driving with them somewhere or doing the dishes together because they don't have to face you. Another possible time for "getting real" conversations could be during family game nights. The kids should be relaxed and happy.

Further discussions might include commitment levels during dating. Emphasize that dating is a time for getting to know many different types of people, and sorting out the kinds of qualities sought in a potential mate. Dating is *not* a time to try out abilities in bed or to discover whether you and your date are sexually compatible.

When our adolescent children begin to socialize (or want to date), we insist that they spend regular time with us, both in and out of our home, and we coach them along the way. We invite their bio-parents to our home, discuss their and our expectations, and exchange phone numbers. The kids, of course, hate this! But this way there's much less chance of misunderstandings or "accidents."

Many teens are restricted from dating until they reach a certain age, say 16. Then their parents tell them in effect to go ahead and jump into a car and have a good time! There is no progression and little instruction. Few behavioral expectations are set. These parents are the ones who are surprised when the police pick up their child for alcohol possession, or their daughter comes home pregnant. We much prefer to supervise and teach.

Our dating discussion isn't complete, however, without the mention of possible restrictions regarding foster children. The offspring of other people must be given special consideration. You may have some limitations concerning the amount of freedom you can give them — as imposed by the court, an agency, or their biological parents. The dating lessons must be adapted to the specific needs of the teens.

If appropriate, ask for a meeting with the bio-parents and your foster child's therapist or caseworker. There you can clarify and set standards, then work out an understanding. All the adults must be "on the same page" for effective parenting and support. Only then can you go ahead with your teaching.

Children from dysfunctional families (or "system children" as we sometimes call them) often have seen far too much of a sexual nature, or may even have been sexually abused. Therefore, they may not have much of a picture in their mind of the correct ways to behave. They also tend to have few boundaries and little self-respect. In some cases, these traits may be so pronounced in your teenage foster children that they shouldn't be left alone with other children. You must be sure they're chaperoned at all times. And you must repeatedly spell out your expectations to them. You also must be careful to alert other adult supervisors of their problems, while keeping details of any abuse confidential. Many questions and answers and checks and rechecks must be done. Girls (and boys) who have been sexually abused may be very damaged and very needy. They should not baby-sit, ride in cars alone with adults of the opposite sex, date without supervision, or go to unchaperoned events. You should feel free to go and check on them, anywhere they are, and correct anything that needs to be corrected. *Parenting is not passive. It is difficult, active, and often tiring.* But the results are worth it!

Before leaving the topic of sexuality, we need to look at two final issues: homosexuality and masturbation.

Homosexuality is a very common area of behavior in foster kids. Sometimes, in fact, it's the reason their parents have "thrown them out"! And masturbation is common among the majority of teenagers.

To begin, I'll mention a difficult situation I encountered several times as a caseworker. I worked with a few foster parents who were very zealous Christians, following "fundamentalist" principles and voicing extreme views and criticisms to their foster children. Homosexuality and masturbation were included in the parental litany. Foster parents are different from adoptive and biological parents in that they must *not* be imposing *extreme* religious views or any other extreme beliefs on children in their home.

Adults certainly have a right to their beliefs. However, they do *not* have a right to impose *religious* beliefs on other people's children. It makes me very uncomfortable to hear foster parents openly condemn their foster children for things like homosexual behaviors or masturbation. To some, the Bible is clear on these matters. To others, the biblical message regarding both topics is not nearly so clear. Remember: There's a big difference between demanding certain *beliefs* and requiring certain types of *behaviors* in your home or in public.

It's counterproductive to belittle a child, criticize their bio-parents, or punish them for normal curiosity or exploration. And it's harmful to harshly condemn children who have already been hurt. If you have such strong opinions that you use them to hurt children, you need to discuss such sensitive topics as these with your caseworker or therapist. Remember, these foster children are *not yours!!*

In fact, I'll make it stronger: ***If you are unable to accept sexualized behaviors, do not take teens who are in the foster/adoptive system!***

Among therapists, social workers, and others who work with children it is well-known that many adolescents not only masturbate but also do a limited amount of same-sex exploring. Most professionals consider these things ***normal*** areas of teen questioning and even exploration. This does ***not*** necessarily mean, however, that they're considered acceptable ***behaviors*** — at least in certain settings. It's crucial to understand the difference.

As noted earlier, the hormones in many teenagers are coursing through their body at high rates and unstable levels. In addition, some conditions such as Attention Deficit Hyperactivity Disorder (ADHD) create tension and discomfort for them. These factors often lead to a great desire/need for sexual activity. When you compound this with high emotional need for acceptance and love, a history of sexual abuse, or an emotional condition like high anxiety, many of the kids feel like a bomb waiting to explode! But learning impulse control is part of growing up — and teaching it is part of what it means to be a parent.

Some teens become promiscuous, and most masturbate. Some try out drugs or alcohol. Others find outlets in sports or similar activities. Calm down, parents. "This too shall pass."

Teenagers are doing a lot of self-assessment. If they have strong feelings for another person of the same gender, they "wonder" if they may be homosexual. A few even "try it" in various degrees, which range from walking differently, to changing their hairstyle, even to putting on makeup (boys). They may experiment with behaviors from mere touching to outright sexual interaction. This doesn't mean they're gay! They also may be exploring things with opposite-sex teens, but we adults tend to think of that as much more normal. They're also trying on other things for size: political beliefs, religious styles, types of clothing, etc. They do this in their normal developmental stage of finding out who and what they really are — and will be as adults. In some cases, of course, acting gay is a "passive aggressive" behavior the teens have specifically chosen because they know it will bother their parents more than any other. They use it as their statement of rebellion and individuality. Others may use it as a way of finding a specific crowd who will accept them as "one of us."

I have always supported a parent's right to require appropriate behavior in public or in their home. But our foster care system is a good example of *American beliefs and principles.* As alluded to earlier, the rules expressly forbid *forcing* religious beliefs onto others. In another section of this book I have discussed attendance at church or other religious observances. But we're talking here about sexual behaviors. A large percentage of teens who come into your home will have a high degree of exposure to sex and sexual issues at a young age. You not only need to establish rules of appropriate behavior, you also must model correct behavior yourself. And in certain instances you will need to protect your biological children from some severely troubled teens. (You should have discussed this with your foster care agency prior to taking these children into your home.)

As a foster, adoptive, and biological parent, I had several children in my home who exhibited what appeared to be homosexual traits or said they were gay. I had frank discussions with them about their thoughts and the implications of their actions, but I did not *condemn.* My sense is that most of them were *not* homosexual. (Studies show that about 10 percent of all males and 3 percent of all females are gay or lesbian, respectively.) Of the kids in my home who masturbated, I told them that was a private thing, and I expected them to keep it that way. They were not to discuss it with others and were not to do it in front of others. My counsel to them in this area is now widely endorsed in the therapeutic community, as well as in many religious groups.

I had far *more* teens who were obsessed with the opposite sex and were inappropriate in public with them. I didn't make a distinction between straight and gay. Though sometimes we had heart-to-heart talks about what they were feeling and why they were feeling as they were, I felt my main task was to teach proper *behavior* and, as noted, simply to accept them. My children were taught not to steal, lie, belch in public, pick their noses, or in other ways embarrass me or themselves. They were taught not to hit others and not to talk back to those in authority. My husband and I found that a matter-of-fact and calm approach usually worked the best. And *he* remained calm even though some of those issues affected him very deeply, even repulsed him at times. You can too!

I have spent a great deal of time in this section on sex because it's so important and, yes, complicated. You also need to discuss ***alcohol and drugs*** — and abuse of both. The bottom line, though, is that all of a child's growth stages fit this model of getting the child's thoughts, then talking things through, step by step.

You can state your expectations for small children more simply:

- "Mommy and Daddy know you will share your toys with your friends."
- "It's important to put your things away and never bring your friend's toys home unless their parents tell you it's OK."

In addition to conversations about sex, drugs, and alcohol, you can say how you expect your children — regardless of age — to behave in the following four settings:

- At the dinner table.
- In church or other religious setting.
- At a party.
- In a restaurant.

In fact, if you do, the sex talk soon won't seem strange to them (or uncomfortable to you!). Even such ideas as how you feel about the law and those who enforce it are probably different from the children who are placed in your home. Do you view police as "friend" or "foe"? Do you say "police officer" or "cop"?

Do your best not to be judgmental or critical, but *do* let them know where you stand and what your expectations of them are. The more communication there is about matters of substance, the narrower the gap between expectations and reality.

CHAPTER 9

Motivation
(Or, 'Why Should I?')

Motivation is the key to discipline! There are dozens of discipline programs, hundreds of parenting styles, and millions of kids who are subjected to them. Which program or style is right for you and your children?

* * *

In Chapter 2 you saw that **motivation** was going to be one of the most important factors in the success or failure of you **and** your child. I have fostered hundreds of children and adopted four. The most successful of these experiences involved both the motivation I felt **and the motivation the child felt.**

My first adoption wasn't planned. A friend who worked in court approached me and told me about a "cute little 13-year-old girl, skinny as a rail, with long blond hair." She had been removed from her home for abuse, and her mother appeared at the first quarterly review hearing, ready to rid herself of the court, the child, and the hassle. She requested paperwork to relinquish her parental rights, and the court gladly complied. My friend told me, "You'd love her, Ann. You and she would get along just fine." I laughed and told him I didn't think anyone would let me adopt, as I was single, working, and struggling to make ends meet as it was. He told me to check it out anyway: "What have you got to lose? And the poor kid was just 'thrown away' by her own mother."

I went home, but the image of "the poor kid" wouldn't leave my mind. So I returned to work the next day and got in touch with my agency's adoption worker. We sat down and discussed it, and she told me there were a few details I had to take care of in my own life first, but I certainly could adopt, noting that several other social workers in our agency had already done so.

Well, I knew I should have already dealt with those "loose ends" in my life, so I began to tie them up. But before I had done much, I received a call from the girl's caseworker in the next county. He told me her foster care placement wasn't working out and asked if I was still thinking about adopting. I said I was. He proposed that I take Missy (her real name at *her* request) in foster care, since I was already licensed for foster children, and get to know her. He explained that it would prevent him from having to move her twice if I did decide to adopt — and this plan would give us a chance to get to know each other before I made my decision.

I met with him and read her case file. It was one of the worst abuse histories I had ever read. My heart went out to her. What could I say? She came to live with me that day!

Now, with that beginning, you might think there was little or no motivation to make a successful adoption. But I didn't know that this skinny little kid wanted a "real family" more than anything in the world, and it would be *her* motivation that really kept us going!

Eventually, I filed for adoption and, after a very rocky year, it was finalized. At that time I had many problems of my own. And Missy, of course, came to me with a pile of *her* own. As she began her weekly visits to a psychologist, I came along to work with him on behavior plans and adjustment problems. He would have me in for a few minutes to talk to me about her. Soon, the few minutes stretched into many. As we went on, I began to take up half of Missy's sessions. Soon the psychologist was setting aside an hour for each of us! I didn't realize it at first, but I was receiving therapy too.

Missy and I grew together. We went to that therapist for four years. She was covered by adoption subsidy, and I had half my sessions paid for by insurance. We walked a rough and difficult road, filled with tears, arguments, power struggles, and hugs. I remember the therapist teaching us how to stop yelling at each other and take "time-outs."

I remember arguing with her about which drawer the silverware should be in ("Missy, stop reorganizing my life!"). I remember the time we put her in a psychiatric hospital, and I became angry at the hospital and pulled her back out "against doctor's orders." But through it all, *Missy persevered.* She needed me, and she wanted this family, and she was a survivor.

As I write this, Missy is a happy young mother, working as a pharmacy technician in a chain drug store where she gets wonderful pay and benefits. She lives in the guesthouse on our farm, and she and her beautiful daughter come for visits every day. When I became critically ill in 2002, it was Missy who held the family together — visiting me every day in the intensive care unit, paying the bills, running the errands, doing the shopping, and taxiing the kids everywhere! She saw that my full recovery couldn't happen without her long-term assistance, and she left her apartment to come to the farm to help me. It sounds like a fairy tale, but to me it's proof that there *can* be success in foster care and adoption.

Unfortunately, all adoptions do not end "happily ever after." Of my other three adopted children, one who has severe emotional problems ran away at 16 and lives about 60 miles from us. She won't have anything to do with my husband and me and denies being our child. I see her child (my grandson) only by the good graces of his paternal grandmother. One child has struggled financially, needing both financial and emotional support since leaving our home. And the last one (who was 15 at this writing and facing delinquency charges) has an uncertain future ahead. However, he reminds me a lot of Missy and wants very much to remain with us, so it wouldn't surprise me if this all worked out in the end.

I have discussed the child's motivation; I haven't said as much about mine. Parents take other people's children for a variety of reasons. And both the parents and the children usually have idealized visions of what the entire relationship will be. Often children who are available for adoption picture a wonderful home, a bedroom of their own, "rich" parents who buy them everything they want, TV images of "family," and no more problems for life. Parents see what they think are "normal" children coming into their home. Continuing with the parental vision/"pipedream" ... these children are grateful that they are wanted and ready to be "shaped" by expert parenting into fine, upstanding adults.

The 'Perfect' Family!

As they say in Hollywood ... *Cut!*

Even if your version of "the dream" is less extreme than this, it's hard to imagine the reality of the everyday grind. I have repeated over and over in this book that these kids come to us with problems. *Problems almost always come with the territory.* That's why these children and teenagers need to find a new place to live.

In Chapters 4 and 6, I discuss the fact that our own problems or differences may actually help us parent these children. We're all human, we fail, we succeed. There is seldom a "perfect ending." I must repeat: It is of great importance to carefully examine your motives before deciding to take these steps. As noted toward the end of Chapter 2 (see "bullets"), there are many reasons — conscious and subconscious — why people choose to parent other people's children. What are your reasons?

Perhaps you feel it's your **duty** to take the child. Many grandparents are parenting grandchildren today. It could be due to the death of the parents, drug or alcohol abuse, the parents' inability to nurture or provide for the children, or any other reason. Parenting our grandchildren is not as easy as it once was, because we no longer live in an extended-family situation. We don't usually have the help of the child's aunts and uncles and cousins. We get little respite from the childcare. And, while we all know being a grandparent is one of the most beautiful life stages, most of us didn't count on being one full time! Most of us aren't physically or emotionally as flexible as we were when we were young.

But we do have the advantage of experience and wisdom and patience. And some receive financial assistance from the state. In many ethnic groups and social spheres, it's the **responsibility** of the entire community to raise the child. In this way families take in children because it is the **expectation** of the rest of their community.

Perhaps you see your wish to parent another's child as a **ministry**. Your motivation is an unselfish desire to do God's work, and it is simply a labor of love. When times become difficult, you pray for strength and guidance, and you likely have the support of your religious "family" as well.

Another reason to take in a child may be that **you are unable to give birth to your own children.** You want a normal family, and you look to adoption or fostering to fill an emotional need to nurture and provide for someone — and to have grandchildren and a "full house."

Some adults take in children they have worked with and have either **grown to love or feel sorry for.** Many social workers adopt. They see the circumstances and needs of the child and know there aren't enough homes to fill the need. They also may be the kinds of people who are **caretakers at heart,** and they feel most fulfilled when they're caring for someone.

Do you simply feel a great **sense of satisfaction,** which you can't readily explain, when you know you made a difference in the life of a child?

Some people believe they can "**mold and form**" a needy child into someone special and positive. This is a delicate, double-edged motive that will be addressed in greater depth later.

As you read on, you will learn that, instead of "molding and forming," you can *teach alternate values and hidden keys that can open up choices* to children who will then form their *own* ideas and personality with which to relate to the world. If these children *choose* to make changes, you may have a hand in helping to end the cycle of generational poverty, dependence, and failure these children would otherwise live in and pass on to future generations.

None of these reasons is wrong. The *key to success* frequently is the *strength and intensity of the motivation.* Parents can only know the difficulty of their job after they begin it. Both biological and foster/adoptive parents have a tough "towpath" to travel.

In the case of children old enough to know what they want in life, *they* also must want to make the adoption or the foster placement work. It may be because they're finally *getting their needs met,* or it may be because they're still *dreaming of the perfect home.* But no matter what their reason, if *they* aren't motivated to make the new relationship succeed, no adult will ever be able to force them. And we must face the fact that some are sticking it out because it's *the lesser of two evils* and better than the alternatives.

I know some of these children who are in adoptive homes instead of institutional placements. The homes aren't perfect, but they're a lot better than living with 150 other kids in so-called "residential" settings, which are about as far from "homes" as you can get!

Summing up ... we see that idealism can get us started, and motivation and perseverance can carry us over some rough spots. Now it's time to get through or around the many roadblocks and normal ups and downs of life with other people's children. How do we handle the inappropriate choices that many young people inevitably make?

CHAPTER 10

Discipline and Punishment

Rules of the house

Living with people requires some sort of structure and expectations of behaviors. In most homes there are rules that are clearly stated — such as curfews, bedtimes, and the need to go to school. In addition, there are unstated expectations and "hidden rules" that we take for granted because they evolved as the need arose, then became habit.

But when another person enters your home, he/she will not know either set of rules. One of the initial duties of a foster parent — over the course of the first week or so — is to sit down with the child and list the **stated** rules in your home, as well as the *hidden* rules. Get other family members — and close friends — to help you. However, the hidden rules may be so ingrained that you might not even realize you follow them. Here are some examples:

Stated rules	Hidden rules
Bedtimes	Decent attire at dinner table expected
Dinner times	Hold hands at table while praying
No profanity or vulgarity	Ask before taking food
No pornography on TV, VCR, or Internet	Clear dishes from table after meals
No drug or alcohol use	Use proper grammar
No smoking	Each person uses own towel
School attendance	Hang up bath towel to dry (re-use)
Attendance at religious services	No wrestling or tickling
Wear acceptable school attire	If you want to use washer, put contents into dryer, whether or not they're yours!
Never go into anyone else's bedroom without first knocking and getting their clearly stated permission to enter!	What is finger food? What is not?
No food in bedroom	What to call the mother?
No sleeping on bare mattress (use sheets)	Don't take mail from mailbox. *Mom* gets it!
Make your bed daily	
Do your own laundry	
Dating rules	
Telephone rules	
Curfews	
Rules about ear piercing, hair dyeing	

For a long-term guest or foster child to be welcome, he/she would have to observe some or all of your rules. Most foster children have moved into so many homes and lived in so many different kinds of places that they're pretty adept at learning the rules, both stated and unstated. But it would be far easier for them if you let them know the really important ones up front, such as I've tried to do in the chart on the previous page. Let me caution you against listing dozens and dozens of expectations for them. This is unrealistic. Think of what happens to the school policy manual when they bring it home. (If you don't have children, I'll tell you. It gets tossed, either in the corner or in the trash, and isn't read.) Also remember that most of these children are not skilled readers — or at least don't operate well on written instructions. Rather, they're partial to oral input.

So … I consider the written rules only reminders and know they may never be read (or may be given just a glance). I happen to be a person who operates on a literal basis, and I write everything down. I cannot learn well orally. I must *see it in writing.* But most people aren't like me. You will have to find out the way your family and the individuals in it operate, so you know how to do this. But if you're planning to become a foster parent, the agency that licenses you will probably expect you to provide a list of house rules for them. The way I did it for my group home, which had new kids coming in all the time, was to post things in writing, as discussed in Chapter 6, then reinforce them orally. That way they couldn't say, "I wasn't told," or "I thought you said *seven* o'clock!"

Without the charts, I couldn't remember how each child's attitude had been each day. And I wanted a visible record for the child, for the caseworker (and for myself) to compute their allowance. Virtually all kids say to their parents, *"That's not fair!"* Usually we have to tell them, *"Life's* not fair, honey. I can't help it!" But this time I made it fair, and everyone could see why one child got more allowance than another. Saving the sheets also showed me and the child any progress he/she had made. In addition, patterns emerged. I could see attitudes and work production increase or slow down after home visits, during hormonal changes, during stressful times in the house, and so on.

Here are other types of 'rules' charts ...

HOUSE RULES

Examples of *non*-negotiable rules:

1. We leave location, phone numbers, and ride information for each other at all times.
2. Everyone goes to the church, synagogue, mosque, etc., of one's choice (though in the case of younger children it's the parents' choice).
3. Everyone goes to school unless very ill.
4. We eat meals together, and we *ask* before eating anything between meals.
5. We taste all foods offered before declining any. We call it a "no-thank-you" helping.
6. Mutual respect must be given and received by all.
7. Everyone is part of the family, giving and receiving "to each, according to his/her need ... from each, according to his/her ability." The strongest people do the hardest work, and each receives what he/she needs, despite differences in abilities.
8. *No tolerance for physical violence* — or R-rated CDs, movies, videos, DVDs, pictures, or behaviors.
9. The lines of authority: Bud→Ann→Designee. If no instructions, the oldest child present. For problems involving a foster child, call the agency. For life-and-death emergencies, call 911.

HOUSE RULES

Examples of negotiable rules:

1. Social events and curfews.
2. When and what work must be done.
3. How much allowance you need/earn.
4. What and how severe consequences are on a case-by-case basis.
5. Bedtimes.
6. Sports eligibility.
7. Friends over — or you at their house.
8. Joining things, needing rides.
9. Phone time, computer time, and other shared-use times.
10. What pets you may have.

❖ *If you set up a schedule – follow it.*

Wake-up time is 6:00 a.m.
  (Saturday 9:00, Sunday 7:00).
Chore time is 6:30 a.m.
Breakfast is 6:45 a.m.
Attendance is required.

Bus time is 7:20 a.m.
School starts at 8:05 a.m.
Arrive home at 4:10 p.m.
Chore time is 5:30 p.m.
Dinner is 7:00 p.m.

Give clear expectations …

1. Orally: "You must take out the garbage before you leave for school."
2. In writing (or pictures): *You must take out the garbage before you leave for school.*

And specific consequences ...

1. The amount of time you come home late from a date is the amount of time you must be early on your next date. Example: If you arrive at 12:15 a.m. but had a midnight curfew, you must be home by 11:45 p.m. next time.
2. If your room is not clean before school, you must have it clean before your after-school snack when you come home.

Failure to complete your daily chores can result in any or all of the following:

1. Extra work in barn area.
2. No phone or computer time.
3. Suspended students shovel manure!

Habits, customs, and other information needed while living here

- If you spill it, clean it up. If you break it, replace it. If you dirty it, wash it. Etc.

- "Do unto others as you would have done unto you."

- Ask before using anything that doesn't belong to you: shampoo, combs, towels, games, CDs, clothing, bikes, sporting equipment, etc.

- Plan ahead for rides and events and fees. Give parents time to work it out.

- No high-caffeine drinks like Mountain Dew, Jolt, etc. Not much soda pop or candy. None in bedrooms.

- Read and follow directions on everything.

Another type of rewards/consequences chart ...

REWARD	RULE	CONSEQUENCE
Phone, TV	Make bed	No phone, TV
Praise, A's	Go to school	Shovel/work

Talk it over with the child, getting his/her input on rewards and consequences.

> ### ❖ No matter what else you do ... FOLLOW THROUGH!

'Truth or Consequences'

> ### ❖ *If you state a consequence, and then there's a problem – follow through.*

In every conversation about discipline, parents ask me about lying: *Why do kids lie, and how do you stop it?*

Children and teens lie for many reasons. There's the "self-preservation" lie, which means that when they're asked if they did something and they know they'll face consequences, many of them say "no" automatically. (Think of how you feel when you're stopped for speeding.)

Solution? *Don't ask!* You're inviting a lie if you do. You can confront, if you are sure they did it, or you can tell several kids what will happen if someone doesn't come forward, or you can simply state you are going to impose consequences because … When you, in effect, ask for a lie, you reinforce the behavior *and lose the battle.*

Should you sneak around and try to "catch" them in lies? That is punishment, not constructive discipline. Should you search drawers and violate privacy? *Not until they give you reason to do so.* (Reasons might include being caught with tobacco or drugs, sneaking out at night to see a girlfriend or boyfriend, getting caught stealing, or some other misdeed.) This may sound harsh. However, *any* children could pick up something in your home and take it with them. My own children have a basic right to protection from me, their parent. This includes protection of their possessions. I am not in the habit of rummaging through my children's things. But, in the course of doing foster care, I now know that some children have a compulsion to steal. If I had any reason to suspect this, I told both them and their bio-parents I would be searching their things each time they went for a home visit, as I wanted to know what they brought *in,* as well as what they took *out.* Therefore, no one could ever *accuse* them of stealing, and they would be protecting themselves. In addition, foster parents are required to take an inventory of children's clothing when they're placed in the foster home in order to determine if the child needs anything.

There are some foster parents who feel they must take an inventory every time a child comes or goes. Others choose to limit the amount of clothing and possessions a child brings into their home. Clothing often gets "lost in the wash" or possessions get "borrowed" either *by* or *from* children (especially teens), and this only creates hard feelings and difficult situations between the adults. Sometimes prevention is better than a cure, but — bottom line — this is a very difficult challenge for many of us.

Although some of this may seem to contradict the discussion of "controlling parents" in Chapter 6, a group home for delinquents is very different from a regular foster or adoptive home. The parents in a group home must be controlling and vigilant because the children placed there are delinquents (that is, the placement is often a consequence, like jail). The parents in the group home may need to practice "overkill" because the dynamics of having a half-dozen teenagers together are so different from those of one or two children (teens tend to "gang up" on the adults!). Usually a specific kind of child is placed in that home *for* the structure and vigilance (a child who has demonstrated the need for it by previous behaviors).

So ... don't confuse the group home with a regular family home. The differences might surprise you! Most adults running group homes are already experienced with many kinds of children and many disciplinary techniques. Their home is a kind of bridge between "family home" and "institution." The current discussion is about family settings, which are supposed to be similar to the average biological family.

Should you make yourself aware of where they are, who they're with, and what's in their room? Yes! Now, you ask, how can I do this without sneaking around, following them, and searching their drawers? Well, you can be open about it and *honest yourself.* (You, after all, are modeling the behaviors you want them to exhibit.)

For example, you should be asking where they are going and who they are with, and they should know you will make spot checks on them. Let them know you want their friends to spend some time at your home or go out with your family, so you can get to know them. You don't need to sneak. Call and ask a parent if your child is there — or ask to speak to your child. Or just show up at a dance, a game, or a house where they said they would be and openly state you are checking to be sure that they're safe, that everything is all right, and, yes, that they're where they said they would be.

In fact, you are *expected* to know the whereabouts of any child placed in your home *at all times.* The children in your care need to understand this! Can you imagine how *you* would feel, as the biological parent, if you called your child's foster home and the foster parent had no idea where the child was? And what would the judge's reaction be? The caseworker? So you really have no choice, and you might just as well make the best of it!

Also *let them know* you occasionally go into their room, pick up some dirty laundry, or bring some clean laundry in and put it away. Tell them you check to be sure that they really changed their bed on Saturday and that you open curtains to let light in. Remind them that you will go in and turn off radios or lights that are left on. Tell them that even though it's their room it's your house and it's not only your right but also your responsibility to do these things, just like checking pockets before doing wash. Also spend time in their room *with them* on occasion. I believe the key is honesty and openness here. You have told them. You can be specific (such as saying, "No, I don't read diaries," or something like that). If you are open and honest, they will respect that, and most of my kids did *not* feel invaded because I was not *sneaking.*

As for supervising, I also occasionally open schoolbooks, book bags, and gym bags; read notes I find on the floor or outside their room (to see who they belong to); check under beds and in closets, both for cleanliness and because it's my job as a parent to do so. My very first foster son taught me to do this. He hoarded food! It wasn't until I began noticing the sound of rodents in my house that I started looking around. Since then I've discovered that kids from kindergarten on up leave food and crumbs *everywhere!* Here I was, patting myself on the back because I was such a great parent, and I had squirrels, mice, and roaches in my home! My husband never objects when I open his lunch box to wash it, so why should the kids?

I even ask to see purses or wallets once in a great while (maybe once in six months). Kids love showing their wallets around with each other. You can learn an awful lot by the photos in a wallet, and one day I was surprised to see a large amount of money there — which I later learned was a birthday gift received at the child's last home visit. Am I looking for things like condoms? No. And I make no judgments if I find them (except I would wonder when and where they might be using them). But things that are illegal are different. Children may not have tobacco, illegal drugs, alcohol, or (in some schools) radios and cell phones.

All of our family's phone conversations were in the open where anyone walking through the room could hear them. Visitors had to be in areas of the home other than bedrooms, and parents and siblings could freely go through those areas as needed.

We began this discussion a few pages ago about lies and why children tell them. Another factor: Some kids tell lies because they have been taught to do so. If foster or adopted children have come from a dysfunctional family system, there are probably "secrets" they are supposed to keep, such as alcoholism, drug addiction, or incest. They may be told to answer the phone and tell bill collectors their parents aren't home. (They may even be taught by their parents to steal.) To combat lies, be up front and say you expect them to tell the truth about you and your home — and they're free to tell their caseworkers and bio-parents anything they need to, so long as it's the truth.

Here you must teach what is appropriate to talk about in "public" and what is not. This is a learned social skill. You aren't teaching them to lie, just to keep personal business personal. An example would be not to discuss other foster children's histories with their friends. Another would be not to discuss, outside the home, income issues and family squabbles. In addition, you should instruct all children of all ages about Child Protective Services and who to contact if they are molested or abused. (This also is a good time to teach children when and under what circumstances to call 9-1-1.)

Lies can be told to increase self-esteem and impress people. Children who do this need to learn that it actually *decreases* respect from others if they find out, and lies destroy trust between friends. These kinds of lies are signals to you to explore ways to "boost the children with truth," so they don't have to lie. Teach them a skill that other kids will want to learn; origami and juggling might be examples. Remind them of a talent you admire in them, such as art or music or chess. Point out a personality trait you like — perhaps cheerfulness or thoughtfulness. If they begin to see themselves as someone others would want to know and be with just because of who they are, they won't see a need to fabricate stories to "make people like me."

❖ *Don't make excuses for them.*

Lies can be told when children actually believe their own fantasies. This is part of a developmental stage that occurs normally in most 3- and 4-year-old children. But it also can occur in children with developmental delays, traumatic experiences, and certain personality disorders. It works sort of like this: "If I wish it hard enough, it will really be true." In their mind, the event or statement becomes true, and they aren't lying because they truly believe it themselves.

If it's *not* part of pathology, a parent can help a child to see reality and not criticize, but simply move through the fantasy. If it *is* part of a pathology, a parent should enlist the help of a professional. In some cases, the myth in the child's mind is actually a protection from a trauma too difficult for the child to deal with, and the pain and suffering when the roots of it are faced can be devastating.

In many cases behavior modification programs work well for lying. But you can get tripped up, unless you are very perceptive. Some of my angriest memories from childhood are about being accused of lies I did not tell. Some children react very strongly, as I did, when falsely accused.

Discuss with the family what consequences are appropriate for lying. Then decide what they will be and clearly define them for the children. If you *know* a child is lying, state the consequence in matter-of-fact terms and tone. You might say, "I feel sad that you chose to lie, but since you did, I'm sure you remember that there's a consequence. So, as it turns out, it was your choice to have the following consequence." With as little emotion as possible, state the consequence, like a judge imposing a sentence. Then you and the child go on with life. The child has paid his/her debt and will have a basis for deciding whether or not to lie the next time.

For more on this way of dealing with children's lies and other misbehaviors, check out the "Love and Logic" discipline program of Foster Cline and Jim Fay. They also wrote a book called *Parenting with Love and Logic: Teaching Children Responsibility* (1990).

❖ *Don't pick battles you can't win.*

The escalating crisis

During the life of every parent, there comes at least one crisis — maybe quite a few more than one! If you have never experienced a child-related crisis, you're a rare parent indeed. If you have ever lived with a "systems kid," I can say with a considerable degree of certainty that you either have undergone — or will go through — a crisis. I can almost guarantee it. Of course, there's a wide variety of crises, and we'll give a small bit of attention to some and a great deal of attention to others.

I believe the most valuable thing I ever learned about parenting was how to stop an escalating crisis. I learned this from the therapist who has been dealing with my foster, adopted, and biological children, as well as my grandchildren, for many years, and who has counseled the entire family both together and individually. I have converted his idea to a visual image and believe it can solve 90 percent of the potentially serious conflicts between parents and children.

Either you or an observer will need to analyze the next argument you have with your child. It likely will follow a familiar pattern, escalating bit by bit. The observer may need to help you identify the pattern and the steps you take.

You and your child probably could write the script for the scene below.

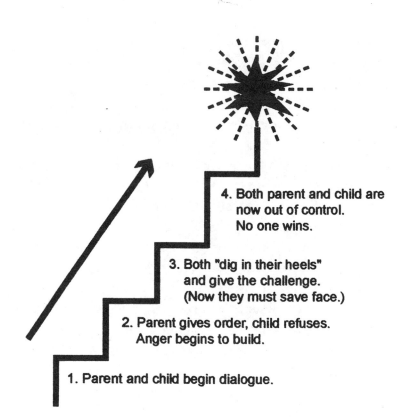

4. Both parent and child are
now out of control.
No one wins.

3. Both "dig in their heels"
and give the challenge.
(Now they must save face.)

2. Parent gives order, child refuses.
Anger begins to build.

1. Parent and child begin dialogue.

The next drawing shows how to *STOP* this familiar scene before it gets to the explosion, as well as how to learn more effective methods of crisis control while dealing with oppositional children.

INTERVENTION

5. Both parent and child are out of control. No one wins.

4. Child is left alone to think and pull things together. (No one must save face.)

3. Parent gives expectation and time limit for child to decide to comply. Parent also gives child consequence in calm voice, then leaves, *allowing time for the ...
GOLDEN MOMENT OF DECISION.

2. Parent gives order, child refuses. Anger begins to build.

1. Parent and child begin dialogue.

New respect and understanding develop between parent and child, and everybody wins!

* If both parties have agreed beforehand, this also may be the moment for a "time-out" for both child and parent, with a plan to resume the discussion at a later time.

Many children, teens, *and* adults have experienced poor impulse control and gotten angry when they shouldn't have. When these times occur between parent and child, it may seem as if there's no way out for either party. By offering choices, consequences, and time to decide, you are allowing mature decisions to be made with a clear head, instead of out of anger and an instinctual need "to win." Some of the most defiant teenagers have complied with my requests when this method was used! No one likes to be out of control, and all of us are given a chance to be *in* control during this type of intervention.

❖ *Don't set up rules or consequences you can't enforce.*

Another type of crisis is a medical one. This is described as a major emergency, such as a person stopping breathing, somehow being poisoned, or experiencing uncontrolled bleeding. In rare cases the child or teenager might make a suicide attempt. Most parents can recognize life-and-death situations and either immediately call 911 or transport the child to the hospital. And foster care placing agencies will give you their policy on handling emergencies when you become licensed.

A word to foster parents here: You are authorized to obtain **routine medical treatment**, such as physicals, immunizations, and office visits for minor illnesses. You also are *required* to obtain treatment for **life-threatening emergencies.** (First, go to the hospital; second, call the agency.) You are *not* authorized to sign for **elective surgery**, non-emergency surgery, ear piercing, tattooing, or other disfiguring or invasive procedures. Even appendectomies must have a parent's signature. You *must* give prescribed medications and may *not* give prescription narcotics or medications that are someone else's without a parent's signature. *You may not put a child on psychotropic medications* (Ritalin, Welbutrin, Paxil, or other mood-altering drugs) without parental permission *in writing.* You cannot diagnose, such as stating, "This child has ADHD." In the case of serious situations, such as appendicitis, if a parent cannot be reached, a judge must sign an order for surgery. For further information, check with your foster care agency. Rules may vary slightly from state to state, but be cautious. As the foster parent, you are liable!

Another type of crisis might be a legal one. Your child may commit an illegal act, may be visited by the police, or might be suspended from school. In all crisis situations, the legal parent and/or agency must be notified. In my experience, documenting the events is the safest, most accurate way to report the incident and protect yourself. Notes jotted down, dated, and filed will help clarify things if anyone needs to review the event. When our adopted son was placed in foster care for a crime he had committed, I began taking notes. For several months my husband and I dealt with the court system, the public and private foster care systems, the adoption subsidy system, the community mental health system, the medical system, and others. If I hadn't taken notes, I doubt that I could've kept it all straight — or in perspective — when going to the court hearings!

If you are parenting a child without legal authorization, you may not even be allowed to be present at an interview by law-enforcement personnel. If you are a legal guardian, you may act as the parent. If you are a foster parent, call the agency. If you are an adoptive parent, *and the adoption has not been finalized yet*, call the adoption caseworker.

The crisis situation most parents face is one of a disciplinary nature. What should you do if a child runs away, assaults someone, gets into a serious verbal altercation, violates a very important house rule, or exhibits threatening behavior to someone? This may be the area that most differs from parenting your bio-child. In today's society, children have *rights* never heard of 50 or even 25 years ago. Depending on the circumstances, that can be a plus or a minus for those who parent other people's children. Foster children cannot be abused physically, sexually, or verbally. Agency rules prohibit the use of any kind of corporal punishment. The old practice of taking a child "out behind the woodshed" no longer exists — certainly not literally and, in general, not figuratively either. So, you ask, what *can* I do? Let's take the examples one at a time.

A runaway child is very common in foster care and adoption. It also may be more common in cases of divorce (running to the other parent), very restrictive and controlling parents (children see no other way out), or children who are taken from their family and placed in a very different type of community from their own.

The first reaction to runaways is to look for them in expected places, such as friends' homes, the other parental home, former foster homes, and so on. You should also look for such clues as missing clothing (they planned it ahead of time), notes (they want to make something happen by running), drugs (they may be afraid and addicted), or any other clue that has meaning to you. Next you should call and report the runaway to the authorities. Law enforcement, a foster care agency, and the other parent(s) are important. His/her friends' parents should be alerted, so they don't unwittingly let the child spend the night or eat there.

It's rather useless to get in the car and go looking for a teenage runaway. Experienced foster parents rarely do. Exceptions:

- In the case of a young child, an immediate search will be launched.
- An older child who has never done it before, has not had an argument with anyone, is not depressed, and has no apparent reason to run would also fall into this category.

Oppositional teens are a different story, however. Defiant teens will hide behind the door, even while their friend tells you with a straight face they aren't there. If you're driving around looking, as soon as they see you they'll jump behind a bush or a building. A chronic runaway, or delinquent, will usually turn up a few hours or days later by getting into trouble with the law. All of these kids must sleep somewhere and eat. Many of them will steal to eat and either go to school or be truant (summer vacation excepted) — and often are picked up at parties or in cars with other teens who are breaking the law. If they have been reported as missing, they almost always will be brought in. Yes, there is cause for worry, but there isn't much you can do. In my state, you will be asked to sign a police report after you give a statement and check the box that states what you will do. For example, will you come to the station to pick up the child? Will you take the foster child back? Will you travel through the entire state (or nation) to pick up the child? Read carefully. You could well be in for a "*no-expenses-paid*" trip to California, Arizona, or Florida!

When making a report about a special needs child, don't forget to state the special needs. For example:

- "This child is under the care of a therapist for depression and may be suicidal."
- "This child is developmentally disabled and unable to function above the level of a 5-year-old child."
- "This child needs medication for diabetes."
- "This child is prone to having unpredictable epileptic seizures."

After the child is picked up and back home, care should be taken to discover the reason(s) for running. This might happen at a "debriefing" session where preventive measures could be put in place, so the incident is less likely to be repeated. If the child has a therapist, he/she should be informed.

Children have many reasons for running away. All human beings are equipped with a safety mechanism in their brain, along with a hormonal system that activates a "fight or flight" response in case of danger — or perceived danger. Thus, children who:

- Feel they have no other way out of a bad situation may run.
- Are being abused may run.
- Have *no other way to get attention or express their feelings* may run.

The italics on the third point are there to draw the attention of parents who may stifle a child's or teen's need to express anger. These parents may not have been allowing any discussion of hurt or fear. They may have been overbearing and appear to the child to be uncaring. Thus, in the absence of an outlet, the child attempts to get away.

The next section describes ways to enlist help with your parenting. I want to emphasize that *all* parents need support systems and help with parenting, not just those with "special needs" children.

CHAPTER 11

The Importance of a Support System

"Why can't I do this, myself?" My friend's question was all too familiar to me. Feelings of inadequacy seem to be very common among parents of children with special needs. They may be foster or adopted children, but biological parents share these feelings too. Any child who is more difficult than most to parent will require help from others to do a good job of parenting. It is no disgrace or failure on their part ... it's just a fact of life with these kids.

* * *

Families may look to the community to form part of their support system. For every foster child I have had, I have sought out a member of my church to mentor the child. This seems to work well for the child, the mentor, and my family (I have never had a chosen mentor say "no" to my request).

Communities can be involved in other ways as well. We have a "Coats for Kids" drive each fall, and I get free winter jackets for my children, so my clothing allowance stretches farther for school clothes. My community welcomes foster kids into such groups as Boy Scouts/Girl Scouts, community choir, school sports, and church. Both you and your licensing worker are encouraged to assess your community to learn where support can be found.

All of us utilize support systems. Some of us are unaware of it, but we humans are communal creatures by nature, not isolated beings. It may be that your family functions largely as its own support system, or you have close neighbors to depend on. Perhaps your synagogue, mosque, or church provides what you need. But those of us who are parenting need more support. And if we're parenting children with special needs, we need a formal, well-developed system to provide for all their needs — *and* the needs of the parents who have taken on a difficult task.

One way to visualize your current support system is to draw it. First, draw a large circle in the center of the page representing you. Next, begin to add smaller circles around the perimeter of your circle and label them with the names of your closest supports, such as spouse, sibling, or best friend. Draw lines to the circles representing the strength of the relationships, such as solid lines (strong) or dashes (not as strong). And finally, draw more circles, representing distant supports you have, such as the Scout group or 4-H club your child belongs to. By looking at the diagram, you can tell where your support system might be weak. This knowledge will help you know which area or areas need to be built up. To illustrate, here's mine as I continue to parent my granddaughter.

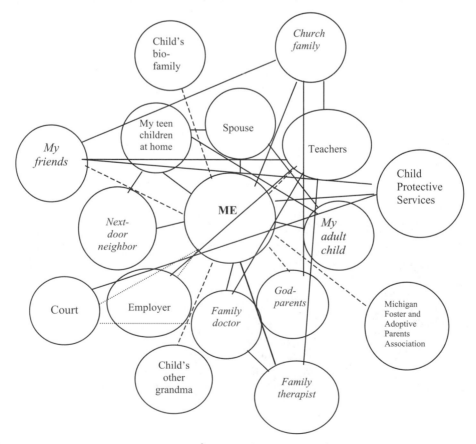

I have drawn a strong line to the family therapist, as I have learned to depend on him after working with him for more than 10 years. I have drawn a weak line to the child's bio-family (meaning her parents) because they are rarely available to assist at all, which is the reason she's with me. You will see that I list Child Protective Services as a strong support. There are two reasons for this. First, CPS has a large file on the child and strongly supports her placement with me. Second, the people in that department are folks I have worked with and have been friends with for many years. Recently one of our older children had to go to court. I couldn't get any information from the prosecutor's office or the court, but I called on a few of my "friends in high places" in other departments, and they "asked around" until they got some information for me. This helped me greatly in getting through the ordeal.

As you can see, I have a large and well-developed support system, and you should too!

If you're having trouble thinking of your support system or group, imagine who you would notify in case of a disaster befalling you or your family, such as a house fire, death, sudden illness, etc. Just place those names in the appropriate circles.

I listed those people who have a part in my granddaughter's life and who could be counted on if she has a need. Depending on the need, I could call on some of them to watch her for me, some to get her to a doctor in an emergency, or some for adjustment issues (therapist, family doctor, teachers, et al.). Next I drew lines of another color to show where those people in my support group interact with each other or overlap. For example:

- Some members of my church family teach in the child's school.
- Some members of my support group are my friends.
- The school where my granddaughter attends employs me as a sub.

With connections overlapping like this, my granddaughter is certain to have many adults concerned about her and interacting often on her behalf.

When one is parenting children with difficulties, a well-organized support group is essential. Usually you don't want to leave your special needs child with "just anyone" in a crisis but with someone who knows his/her history and special needs. When you have trouble — whether physical, emotional, financial, or otherwise — you need people to depend on for help. If the child is severely handicapped, you can*not* parent him/her alone. Don't try!

It takes a great deal of time and energy to form a stable support group. Much depends on the available resources, personalities of service providers, aggressiveness of the parent, and appropriate interaction between and among providers. Here is one example.

A couple moves into a new community with their special needs, adopted child. Since the child has been in special education classes in a previous school district, the new school has been informed, and the parents will need to contact the special ed coordinator in that school. The law says an individual educational planning conference (IEPC) must occur within 30 days to determine if the placement is appropriate. *The parents, however, must arrange for the initial placement!* So they must contact their first support person.

When they talk with this person, they ask for the names of experts in the community who are familiar with the specific disability their child has. For example, is there a doctor who specializes in ADD and ADHD? Is there a psychologist who deals with foster or adopted children on a regular basis? Is there a support group for parents of children with cystic fibrosis? In this way they're building a list of potential support people to contact.

Next they find a family physician, get an appointment, and work out a treatment plan. When they meet with him/her, they ask about the doctor's willingness to supply documentation and communicate with other providers for the child. Then they clarify who will do the coordinating. From there the parents may move on to a therapist, a dentist, a school counselor, or other professionals who need to interact with their child.

Waiting until there's a crisis is not a good idea! People who know the child, the family, and the circumstances should be in place *before* they are needed for an emergency situation. Records have to be transferred from prior service providers, confidentiality releases must be signed, and the parents and support team need to be made aware of each other's name and role.

This can be a demanding process. And it's very important to choose, or at least discover, a group coordinator. Personality has a lot to do with this.

It may be that the child's medical doctor will ask for reports from others for the file, or the child's therapist will schedule meetings with you and others from the team. Perhaps the special education people will send notices to everyone on the team when scheduling the planning conference. At the very least, all members of the team should have the same documents, reports, assessments, and paperwork. It may be up to the parent to see that this happens; only you will be able to tell. But here's another example of how an otherwise negative trait can stand you in good stead. For a parent who is (appropriately) aggressive in advocating for his/her child — and who isn't afraid to take a leadership role — will often get the best service. On the other hand, an easygoing parent who can follow instructions and deal with odd or aggressive personalities can achieve the same thing if another member of the team is the outspoken "leader" type. The expression "The squeaky wheel gets the grease" applies here — within limits, of course.

Some creativity can be used to garner support. I actively seek out a member of my church to be a mentor for each of my special needs children. It almost never does any good to put a notice in the bulletin or stand in front of the congregation and ask for "someone" to help you. Instead, I target an individual who may have the right skills, or someone who seems to have taken an interest in the child, and ask for a *specific favor.* If one is asked a question directly and has already seen a need, it's much more difficult to say no!

For example, I don't like to shop. I detest malls. I am not "fashion minded." So when I saw that our teenage adopted daughter had latched onto a young, married (but childless) woman in our church, I approached her and asked if she would mind taking my daughter to buy her school clothes, if I provided money and covered their lunch. She was delighted to oblige, and it was the beginning of a long friendship between them. I never had to buy school clothes for that particular child again! And the mentoring relationship extended far beyond that service — for both of them. Now that my child is grown, they do many things together and are still friends.

You may find a "buddy" for your child *and* a parent who has something in common with you. My bipolar/ADHD son has a close friend with emotional problems similar to his. The boy's mother frequently goes horseback riding with me. We have become "best friends" too! You may call on a 4-H leader, a Scout leader, a Sunday school teacher, or member of a church's senior high youth group. Our high school requires a minimum number of community service hours for graduation. I have approached the school counselors and asked them to steer in my direction any students headed for a career working with children. We then work out a "community service program" of mentoring, tutoring, or some other activity — and permanent friendships often result. As with my horseback partner and her son, everyone benefits from the experience.

Some members of the support system provide professional services, while others provide support for *me.* There have been some pretty serious crises in my 37 years of parenting, and my own needs sometimes became as important as those of my special children. I have experienced health problems, children's accidents that resulted in life-and-death situations, abuse allegations against me or my home, and other problems. During these times the professionals handled the children, and the "lay people" handled *me!* My church family brought in meals for a full month when I recently lay near death in the hospital. My child's godmother stood by my side when I was being questioned by a Child Protective Services worker after my daughter was run over by a car. My friends from church kept one of my children for three months, during a court process he was involved in. There was even a time when my house caught fire Christmas Eve day and, as I arrived home from work, I saw my minister and other church leaders on the roof placing tarps over the holes the firefighters had put in it! (The wonders of life in a small town will never cease to amaze me!)

A word to the wise for foster parents:

Once you receive your first foster child, you will do your best to apply all you have learned to be the best parent in the world. However, you are *not* expected to do it alone! Do *not hesitate* to call the foster care agency for help, thinking the officials there will see you as a failure. Do *not* wait until you're at the end of your rope, reduced to tears, and "can't do this anymore"! If you have reached this point, there is a great danger you will "break the placement" (ask to have the child removed). No agency or caseworker wants this to happen. They *want* to support you. They *expect* you to have questions. They *anticipate* that you will be learning and growing as time passes. For the benefit of the child and yourself, seek help early and build successes, not failures, in the beginning of the placement. You are not a "failure" or an "inadequate foster parent" just because you ask for help!

Bottom line: A support system is not only "nice" to have, it can be a lifesaver, as it has been for me.

CHAPTER 12

Learning from the Wisdom of Others

Children in the foster and adoptive systems have special needs and have lived in pain for most of their life before you meet them. It usually takes a great deal of knowledge, physical and emotional stamina, and almost constant supervision to help them through life. No one individual can be expected to have all these abilities. Convincing foster and adoptive parents to enlist help from others is therefore very important. Caseworkers can help prevent burnout, marriage instability, and feelings of failure in their foster homes by helping parents build support for themselves.

* * *

If you have a child with a specific mental or physical disorder, you may be able to join a support group in your community. If your child is foster or adopted, there will be a support group through your agency or a multi-agency coalition. Join it! Not only will you make new friends in the new town, you also may be a support person for someone else who needs it, and there may be a day when you need that support yourself.

Why do I recommend this? The members of such a support group may have gone through the same kinds of things you are going through. They may be able to provide suggestions and aids to ease life with a difficult child. "Why reinvent the wheel?" is an old saying that means someone else has already solved that type of problem, so why waste your energy doing it all over again?

I have listened closely to other adoptive parents when they talk about adoption subsidy, services available, pitfalls of adoptions, and the jungle they have tried to hack their way through — the jungle called the "adoption system." It taught me much. I have attended conferences on attention deficit disorders, talked with other adults who have it (or have children with it), and compared notes and funny stories. There are many problems inherent in raising children with certain disabilities and diseases, and you just might benefit from some moral support from those who have "been there." Try it!

Sometimes people have negative experiences in fostering or adopting, and the result may be a great deal of pain for everyone involved. If you go to a support group or "hang out" with others who foster and adopt, you might be able to avoid the same pitfalls. (Just don't allow yourself to get bogged down in the "horror stories.")

What experiences am I talking about? Well, in a way I'm reluctant to mention them, because I don't want to dissuade you from fostering or adopting, but another adage is "Forewarned is forearmed," so I'll forge ahead!

If you recall, I spent a great deal of time earlier on the matter of assessing yourself and the child you're thinking of taking. Suppose a potential adoptive child has a history of violence or assault? You assess your family, pray or think about it for a time, discuss it with the caseworker, and take him anyway. Then you hear from a member of an adoption support group that a similar child assaulted her biological son, beat him up, and stole her car. *Oh my!* Will this happen to you?? There are no guarantees, but it probably won't happen if you take certain precautions against it.

For example (as noted in Chapter 8), I never left my young children with a foster or adopted child as a baby sitter. Why? Usually they're in the system because their parents didn't know how to parent, and they had no one to teach them. So could they parent my child? Maybe so, maybe not. I didn't want to take that chance. I also never left car keys anywhere in the house that could be taken by a child or teenager. They stayed in my pocket or locked in my bedroom, and all spare keys were locked in my husband's gun safe. And our children weren't told where the keys were hidden.

Do you have a child who steals? Don't leave money lying around in obvious places — like nightstands, dressers, or even in your purse. That's the first place they look. Even though I have retired from fostering, I still carry all my cash in my pockets, just from habit. I *told* all my children there were no credit cards or cash in my purse and made no secret of taking money out in front of them — from my pockets. I sometimes asked them to get a comb, a nail clipper, a pen, or something else from the purse, so they would *know* there was no money there. Why tempt fate?

Do you take — or are you considering taking — female, teenage foster children? Be sure there is a well-known house rule that no female is *ever* alone with *any* male in the house. If my husband picked one up from school, he took another child along. If I went out shopping, I took the girl or found a sitter. If I was out, my husband did not sit around watching TV with one girl in the room. This protects everyone involved, so that the likelihood of anything improper occurring is greatly reduced.

Others who have traveled "the road" can give you a great deal of wisdom as well — some through that often painful 20-20 hindsight — and you'll do well to listen to their advice. It can save you a lot of grief.

So, you may say … You tell us all about the bad things, the need for support, the scary things. Aren't there any good things we can learn from others?

You bet! I'm still learning, even though I quit fostering — and no longer run a group home. Open your ears and eyes and you will hear some wonderfully creative things.

From me, you will hear that every experience should be a learning experience. From another friend, you may learn ways to bring out the best of your child's creativity. You may hear, as I have, that you can celebrate each child's heritage by:

- Cooking ethnic foods they like.
- Decorating your home for Christmas or Hanukkah or Kwanzaa as they do wherever they came from.
- Reading stories about people just like them.

You may discover that your child is an artist, a poet, a musician, a sports enthusiast, a mechanical whiz, or a computer expert. When you discover that a friend or acquaintance has similar interests — or has a child with those hobbies — your child and that adult or youth can get together for their mutual benefit and enjoyment.

How can you work well as a team member? You can supply all the information your caseworker needs, get the children's dental and medical exams on time, invite workers for lunch or coffee occasionally.

Want more ideas? One of my fondest memories of raising my children is our annual "Fall Harvest" party. All foster and adoptive children — and all our grandchildren or anyone who wanted to come — were invited. We (family and friends) cleaned out our huge barn, decorated with a fall theme, readied the ponies and wagon, and threw a huge party. The foster/adoption agency did the games, the parents brought potluck food, I drove the wagon for the hayride, and the kids supplied music. We did anything and everything that was traditional for a "fall" party, like bobbing for apples and taking the hayride. We also had games for little kids, activities for teens, and lots of social interaction for parents. Since the parents involved with both a private agency and the state agency came, it served as a great interface for personnel and parents, and a splendid time was had by all.

What about ideas for holidays? I once had a child whose parents were deceased, and he was in permanent foster care. I invited his grandparents for Thanksgiving Dinner and got in touch with his biological sister in another foster home in another town. She came too. After we asked the blessing, the grandparents began to cry. They told us that for all the years "Bobby" had been in foster care, we were the first family who had ever included them in his life. When "Bobby" left us, he went to live with those grandparents. Since he was handicapped, this turned out to be just the support system he needed when he left the foster care system.

Other good things to do with young people are making "life books" or scrapbooks, playing games, spending individual time with them, and doing all the other things you can read about in any good parenting book.

So, you see, you can continue learning from other parents all the time, then apply the best ideas to your own parenting style and techniques.

CHAPTER 13

Fostering: 'If I Had Only Known'

In Chapter 12 we listened to the voices of experience and looked at some of the pitfalls and joys that often are "part of the package" with foster and adopted children. In this chapter I'll be even more specific — in an attempt to prepare you for both the bad and the good, thereby giving you a clearer picture of what may be coming down the road on this great adventure!

There are certain behaviors common to many foster children. Your licensing worker should go over them with you and ask which ones you absolutely can*not* live with. This will help them know which types of children not to place in your home. A partial list is given here:

- History of lying.
- History of stealing.
- Acting out before and after visits to bio-home.
- Making virtually no effort to connect with family where one is living.
- Damaging one's home.
- Not taking care of possessions.
- Eating far too much junk food/sugar.
- Poor grammar, reading, spelling.
- Behind in school, at least one grade.
- Pattern of defiance.
- Hyperactivity (unless depressed).
- Bedwetting.
- Poor manners.
- Poor hygiene.
- Inappropriate behavior in public.
- Pattern of running away.
- History of violence.
- History of arson.
- History of being abused.

There are many more things some foster children do, but the licenser should show this list to you, and you should decide between you and your spouse if you want to handle these kinds of troubled children. In addition, your training classes should give you some ideas to utilize when dealing with these problems. Don't be afraid to ask questions, and don't be afraid to refuse certain kinds of children. There are lots and lots of kids out there who need homes, and they need all different kinds of parents. You will be able to fill the need in some way. No one will be upset with you — and you needn't feel guilty in the slightest — if you decline to take a violent child, a fire-setter, or a child who has sexually abused others. Let the more experienced foster parents deal with these kids, or let the institutions handle them. Don't destroy your own family by overloading yourself from the very beginning.

Another thing to mention in a chapter titled "If I Had Only Known" is the issue of caseworkers and their role. You will learn that you must ask them for help. If you never call them they think everything is going fine, and they will "put out fires" elsewhere. Remember when I said how much turnover there is among caseworkers? If you have been a foster parent a year or more, you might know more than they. But they do know about, and have access to, "the system" and may be able to access funds for special needs or other "perks" for you or your child. For example, most of them have a book of community agencies and resources; they can steer you to people in service clubs and other helpful agencies. Many such organizations are able to send your child to camp at no cost to you. They should know where to get more clothing (your clothing allowance is inadequate to say the least). For example, all children who have a Medicaid card can get free clothes from our "Clothing Closet" located at the social services agency.

Good-hearted people in most communities are looking for "poor" kids to donate Christmas gifts to, and the caseworker could submit your child's name to them. Social workers know emergency procedures, complaint procedures, and reporting procedures. *Ask!*

I used to get very nervous when the foster care worker came out to visit the child. In my state there's a requirement that every worker visit every child *in the foster home* at least once a month. I always worried about the messy house and what my foster child said to the worker when they were talking privately. But one day about 10 years into the game I learned a very important truth: *They need you!* Without foster homes, they have no jobs. Without foster homes, there will be no kids *to* worry about. *And* they know you are just an average human, with faults and assets, and they won't worry about such little things as a dirty house — unless it's a danger to a child because it is *so* dirty or unhealthy.

The child may say you yell at him. So? Most parents do! If the child alleges cruelty or physical harm, you should worry, but unless you do that, why would the child say it? (False allegations *do* occur, but your licensing worker will sort through them.) At any rate, most social workers learn very quickly the things children say that are true and those that are manipulative or false.

Speaking of reports, remember to document everything. Any paperwork you can give the caseworker will be of assistance to him/her in writing that report. It could also help you. Many states rate the amount of subsidy you get according to the level of difficulty of the child. If you don't document problems, defiance, number of calls from the school, and so on, you may not get the additional subsidy you should have coming to you.

Another reason to document is to find patterns in behavior. For example, children often act differently just before or after visits to their bio-home. Or a girl may get depressed and nasty about once a month. You could help her to understand why, as well as providing proof for her doctor that she may need treatment for premenstrual syndrome.

I have stated it before, but I will restate it for its importance: Know how much you can tolerate and *have a list of rules and consequences.* In the discipline chapter I stated that you should not "write a book" of rules. Just jot down some and go over them with the child. Others can be told in the next day or two, but don't wait too long! As schoolteachers also realize, it's a lot easier to ease up than to tighten up — if change is needed.

If you deal with biological parents, you would do well to document everything. You can get caught in a trap of "he said, she said" — and messages can be twisted between bio-parent and caseworker and between child and you. Remember that many parents are angry because the court removed their children. They may want to take it out on you because they think the court believes you are a better parent than they are. It's better if you can make friends, perhaps even becoming a mentor for them after the child returns home.

If you're thinking of adopting your foster child, check into the adoption subsidy rules. It's another maze to get through, but it's vital to do so. In some states all subsidy stops when you adopt. In others, it carries on at the same rate as the foster care money (Tip: Get the highest rates you can *before you adopt*. Rates, once set, are hard to change.)

Know before you adopt that some of your family and friends won't support you. Some may even shun you. Be prepared to make new friends *and* be less welcome in the homes of some of your old ones. Be grateful for any family support.

Be sure you aren't an "enabler." Do nothing to support bad behavior but also do nothing to hide it from caseworkers, teachers, and police officers. It will only hurt the child in the end. If you haven't heard about the concepts of co-dependence and enabling, discuss both with your licensing worker.

❖ *Reward good behavior.*
❖ *Support kids when they're right.*

Another issue in the "If I had only known" category is adoption subsidy.

Adoption subsidy in my state (Michigan) continues at the same rate as the foster care rate. Therefore, as I said previously, you should try to have it set as high as possible before adopting. Second, adopted children are eligible for a medical subsidy and Medicare. This may become very important if your child acts out and gets in trouble with the law. It also will be needed if your child is hospitalized or institutionalized for any reason. Be sure you carefully review your prospective subsidy with your adoption worker and understand it thoroughly before going ahead with your adoption. It's especially necessary in adoptions of older children, as they're likely to need interventions — and the medical subsidy will pay for them.

Adoption subsidy varies from state to state. The highest-subsidy states are currently Michigan, New York, and California. Lower-subsidy states tend to be in the South or less-populated areas in the Plains. When my third adopted child ran away, I learned that the adoption-subsidy check is sent *ahead of the month it is for*, and the foster care checks are sent *after the month you have had the child*. The significance of this for me was that I had been paid for the entire month, and she ran away on the second day of the month, so *they wanted my money back!*

Allow me to emphasize: It is of great importance to discuss subsidy with your adoption worker, so that you thoroughly understand it. Subsidy is rarely paid for a baby, unless there are medical needs. Subsidies do encourage the adoption of special needs children; they also may assist in grandparent or other relative adoptions. In Michigan, subsidy and foster care payments aren't considered income and don't have to be declared on tax forms. They are considered reimbursement for expenses you have while raising the child.

It's hard to say what you might need to know and not tell you 5,000 irrelevant things to protect you from harm or sadness or a broken placement. This is another reason that a network of support (see Chapter 11) is so essential — and that mentorships have become so popular.

On one occasion, I accidentally learned something very valuable: what my caseworker's job was. When I became a foster care worker and understood the role and responsibilities of the job better, I was far better at both helping my caseworker and getting things for my child.

For example, caseworkers loved my monthly reports. I e-mailed them information about school progress, home behavior, therapy and medical progress, dental visits, and anything I considered helpful or pertinent. Why did they love them? Because they have to write a quarterly report and give a progress report for each child on their caseload. A thorough report by you on your child makes their job much easier. I discovered that sometimes workers simply used my report instead of writing the narrative part themselves.

And, if you don't like to write, simply call and leave messages on the phone. An example would be something like this:

Hi, Jodi. This is Ann Stressman, reporting on my foster son, Jon Jones, for the month of October. Jon passed all his mid-term exams, has a "C" average, and has had no behavior problems in school. He had his eyes checked and needs stronger glasses, which we ordered. I'm mailing in his dental form. He had two minor cavities. Jon's mother and I talk by telephone at least weekly, and she is supportive and cooperative. In Jon's Independent Living program at high school, we're working on the "healthy foods" unit. He plans one meal a week, shops for it, and cooks it. He's learning fast and needs very little help from me. As for money handling, I could not convince Jon to save for a long-term goal, such as a car or an apartment, but he did agree to save for a Super Nintendo XBox and Gamecube — and when he has enough money, we'll go shopping. I believe his next court date is not until after the holidays. Give me a call if I have left anything out. Thanks! Bye.

Other ways to assist the caseworker include driving the child to appointments, taking care of annual medical and dental exams, getting forms turned in on time, and learning to deal with minor crises and common behavior problems (instead of calling too often for help).

So ... now you have joined forces with another member of the team, and things are going well.

For many foster parents, another question eventually surfaces: to adopt or not to adopt?

CHAPTER 14

Adopting:
Knowing What's Right for You

"The trouble with a kitten is that
Eventually it becomes a cat."
            -Ogden Nash

Since this isn't a book on adoption per se, but on parenting, I'll be brief in the "deciding" section. If you have read the preceding chapters, you now know there is more to parenting a "special" child than meets the eye. We have looked at core issues like the influences of environment on the first days and months of a child's life (indeed, even the days and months before the child is born). We discussed the impact that living in poverty has on learning styles, discipline, values, and behavior. And we have taken a hard look at ourselves, our assets and liabilities, our motivation, and our level of commitment. So what's left? Well …

When people adopt a dog or a cat, it's a commitment to care for that animal for an average of 12 years. Yet many of those people end up giving away the animal, leaving it out in the country, allowing it to roam the streets where it can come to harm or create unwanted offspring. When people bring the cute puppy or kitten home, they don't expect things to end up that way, but all too often it happens.

❖ When you adopt a _child_, you are making a _lifetime_ commitment!

Adopting a child, of course, involves far more than daily feeding and annual trips to a vet! Your pre-adoption assessment is critical, and your level of commitment will determine the success of the placement. From a legal standpoint, one's responsibility to an adopted child in the United States ends when the child reaches age 18. But, as with all of our children, our moral obligation to the adopted child continues for "as long as you both shall live"!

There may be a lot of choices to make, or you may have to accept a narrow range of possible children. At this writing, the scarcity of healthy Caucasian babies in the U.S. is unbelievable. Waiting lists at agencies can stretch into nine or 10 years! Even healthy babies of other races are becoming more and more rare, because so many young girls are choosing to bring their babies home and raise them as single parents. Also, abortion and birth control have taken their toll on the "available" population, so that many prospective adoptive parents become frustrated and start feeling hopeless. Others decide to widen their range of possibilities and accept cross-racial placements, medically fragile infants, drug babies, sibling groups, and older children. They know that by doing this they won't be waiting in line (at least such lines tend to be rather short), but usually they can get a child fairly soon. This is not without risk, however!

You must decide what is right for you. Can you accept an older child, with an individual personality, quirks, differences, and difficulties? Will you be proud of your different-race child when out in public? Are you able to work with mental or emotional problems? These are hard questions, and there are no easy answers. Raising special needs children can be rewarding, or it can be destructive to both parents and children. I'll give a few anecdotes, gleaned from my years as a caseworker and my association with adoptive parents throughout my state and community. (The names are changed.)

"Susie" was a client of mine when I first began working in outreach crisis intervention. She had been adopted as a baby and knew it. Her adoptive parents' marriage had remained intact, they lived a comfortable middle-class lifestyle, she had an older adopted brother, and she had very conscientious parents. But Susie was in crisis! She was acting out at home, her grades were sliding at school, and the crowd she hung out with wasn't exactly the bring-home-to-dinner variety. Susie fought constantly with her brother "Michael" and her parents. When I met her she was planning to run away. What was her problem?

Susie's appearance was clearly that of a biracial child. She had light skin; dry, frizzy hair; dark eyes; full lips; and a broad nose. Her general appearance was African American. A beautiful and intelligent girl, Susie was filled with anger and frustration and a terrible sense of betrayal. Why? Although it was obvious to her and anyone else looking at her that she was biracial in color and features, her parents kept insisting she was "French Canadian and entirely Caucasian." She was angry at the lie, angry at not really knowing who she was. She wondered what else they had lied about during the years she had lived with them. Her brother wasn't mixed-race, but she was. And since her parents wouldn't admit the truth, they couldn't discuss it. So Susie felt she had no one at home to support her in her curiosity, to talk with about her identity, or to teach her about the other half of who she was.

Well, we did some short-term crisis intervention, referred her family to a good therapist, and hoped for the best. I recently met Susie again at a store. She looked healthy, happy, and self-assured. And she was pregnant! She recognized me first and quickly gave me a hug. She tried to tell me about 10 years in one minute; her words fell over one another. The counseling had helped. Her parents had finally admitted the true nature of her bio-parentage. Though she had looked briefly for her bio-parents, she hadn't found them. Susie was now married to a wonderful man, they had a home in a town near me, and they were expecting their first baby in two months. She had graduated from high school and had a good job — and her husband was steady and faithful.

"Wow! We made it!" I said. She agreed, and we both recalled how rough it had been. I see her once in a while in that store and remember how one issue had turned her life into utter chaos — and nearly cost those parents the joy of becoming grandparents.

In another adoptive home, a single mother with three children began the process of adopting a fourth child, a girl, who was older than those she already had. Six months after the older child moved in, she began sexually abusing the other three children. When one of them finally told the mother, the reporting child did not reveal the true extent of the abuse or the duration. The adopting mother requested placement for her child in a mental hospital, along with a thorough evaluation to help determine how likely it was that the behavior would be repeated. Therapy sessions began in earnest, and the stress of deciding whether or not to complete the adoption was agony. At the time the mother didn't know the extent of the sexual contact; the children presented it as if it were a childish game. Despite some misgivings, the woman eventually went ahead with the adoption, and the teenager didn't repeat the behavior. She is now a self-supporting adult and a great asset to her aging mother.

Still another acquaintance of mine and her husband adopted five different children in the space of two years. They were adorable, young, and very lively kids. They were a variety of races and ages, and a challenge because of their high-energy behavior. My friend adores babies and young children! Elementary children are her passion (she's a school social worker in an elementary school). But she doesn't relate nearly as well to teenagers! I'm worried about the increased difficulty she and her husband will encounter when those five children are teens and perhaps not as likable as they were in their younger, "cuter" years. It's the kitten/puppy syndrome all over again, but now the stakes are higher. These are real, living, breathing human beings. Will she be sorry she adopted? Will she be able to cope? Will the kids be manageable? I guess we won't know the answers to those questions for several more years.

The open adoption

It may surprise you to know how common open adoptions are nowadays. You also may find that babies aren't available in your community, unless you're willing to accept some degree of openness in your approach to adoption.

There are, however, many degrees of open adoptions along the continuum, and you will be the one to decide how much you can live with. This is something your adoption worker can work at with you, but the adopting parent is always in control.

Here are a few examples.

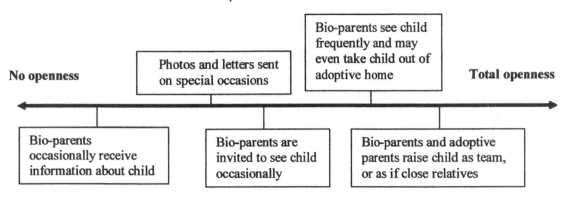

Whether you pursue an open adoption or a more traditional one — and when*ever* you take in a foster child — you will need to work with a "system." This system inevitably will have red tape and bureaucracy, but it also will have caring people trying to do the right thing by children and families. Building positive working relationships with people at all levels of the system (or systems) is essential to your mental and emotional health, as well as that of the children who are becoming part of your life. Good relationships with people in the "system" also enhance the chances that placements with you and your family will be successful.

We'll take a look at these factors in the next chapter.

CHAPTER 15

Systems Issues/Establishing Working Relationships

*Another important topic that must be addressed is one I call "system issues." This topic alone could fill a whole book! But if you and your partner are parents of a foster child or take an adoptive placement, you **will** deal with the "system." Even if you take in a relative's child, you may find you need to have "legal guardianship or custody" in order to obtain medical care or register the child in school. Gone are the days when a boy could simply live down the road with another family because those folks needed help on the farm or his parents were struggling.*

*What "system" am I talking about? Well, more accurately, it is "systems." Raising a child in the 21st century requires that you interact with a medical system, a school system, perhaps a social welfare system, or maybe an agency. Many examples could be cited, but in general foster and adoptive parents are required to keep medical records, legal documents (such as birth certificates), and many other types of paperwork on any child in their home. When you have a child with special needs, you will likely encounter a special education system, a court system, additional medical or charitable organizations, mental health systems, and others too numerous to name. As we continue making our way through this book, you will find tips on how to make it a little easier to find **your** way through these "dense forests" of paperwork, red tape, rules, requirements — and the bureaucrats who interpret them!*

* * *

Placement services and your family

Usually foster children are placed in homes through the state's social welfare agency or a private agency that contracts with the state to do foster care. In other areas, community mental health agencies may place — for either long-term or respite placements. In different states there are different names for the state agency, but they serve the same function. Yours may be the Family Independence Agency, Department of Social Services, Health & Human Services, or another name. Many private agencies throughout the United States and the world supervise foster care placements. Each state also has different rules for foster parents, and within the private agencies there also may be different requirements.

To further complicate matters for the aspiring foster parent, there are many different kinds of foster care. Naming several will illustrate the confusing issue (see Appendix H for greater detail):

- Medically fragile children.
- Pregnant and parenting teens.
- Pre-adoptive placements.
- Delinquent youths.
- Neglected or abused children.
- Therapy homes.
- Group homes.
- Emotionally impaired children.
- Physically impaired children.
- Independent living placements.
- Shelter care placements.

Of course, there are even more, if you include secured and unsecured detention, residential care, adult foster care, and mental health hospitalizations! So if you're new to foster care, don't be bashful about asking questions.

Most people have an idea of what they want to do when they apply for a license. Usually parents start doing that, or they can gradually work into a specific kind of placement. Most homes take *either* boys or girls, but not both. (Because of this, sibling groups often must be separated.) Shelter care usually means emergency placements, for 30 days or less, while the child is evaluated or awaits a court hearing. In my county in Michigan we also have placements of two weeks or less for a crisis-intervention program. If you want to do foster care, call a private or state agency and ask for information. When I moved across a county line, I asked my agency who had the most teenagers for placement and ended up switching to the agency that did.

In many states foster care is tied closely to adoption. Infants may be placed in pre-adoptive care, either in a separate home or in the adoptive home. Foster parents may adopt children they have had in foster care — if the state terminates the children's bio-parents' rights. Some people sign up for foster care in order to get to know the kinds of children they may get for adoption, or in hopes of getting long-term placements who might end up being eligible for adoption.

Payments differ widely from state to state. In the more populous states — such as California, Michigan, New York, or Florida — payments may be higher than in such states as Idaho and Montana or the South. But payments aren't to be used as an income. They are a subsidy, paid to compensate the foster parents for care they have rendered. There's such a wide variety of methods and amounts that it isn't possible to list them all here. But it is important to understand the payment system in your state and how to handle it on your income-tax statement (*not* income, remember?).

Another issue to consider is whether you get to keep the subsidy payments if you adopt, or do they stop? In my state the subsidy doesn't change. It was set up that way to encourage adoptions and *permanency* for the child. In some states parents lose their subsidy if they adopt. Thus, there are fewer adoptions. This does a disservice to the child, who deserves a permanent family.

A word must be added regarding the perceptions of family, friends, and the public as to the motives for fostering or adopting. On the surface it may appear that foster parents are receiving a large check each month for sheltering a child. However, even in a state that pays higher-than-average rates, a different perspective reveals the reality.

The rate is usually less than $1 per hour for a job that requires responsibility and supervision 24 hours a day, seven days a week.

Although many people in the service professions choose their vocation or job *both* for the income and for the kind of work they feel drawn to, foster care providers can't earn enough income doing foster care to support them and their family! They also need other income. In addition, it should be noted that foster children frequently need help with schoolwork, psychological counseling, and transportation to the agency for parental visits. Further, if a child is diagnosed with a learning disability or personality disorder, medication and special education services may be necessary.

Wraparound services

You may or may not recognize the term "wraparound services." It is a concept our social services system uses to assist families who enter the system because they are having problems. A team is formed to provide the different kinds of services the family needs and to both analyze the family and advocate for it. Frequent meetings take place, and the family is an integral part of the treatment goals.

For example, a team may consist of a foster care worker, a homemaker, a tutor, a probation officer, a substance abuse counselor, a special education coordinator, a mental health worker, and a coach or teacher from school. The intent is to coordinate and address all the needs of the family and not just focus on the "identified patient" who came into the system as a result of one or more specific incidents.

Foster care and adoption workers

Occasionally you get a "veteran" social worker or a child who has been in the system for many years. It is those individuals who know how to get what they need from the system. If other states are like mine, however, caseworkers average only a year in foster care, and the goal for children is 6-12 months. Therefore, you might want to ask for a mentor who has fostered for a long time so that you can get advice on how to more effectively advocate for your child — and how to obtain those things they need. The system is a typical bureaucracy and can be difficult to wade through, but if you learn to deal with it, you can do wonderful things for children.

There are many books on adoption, so we'll just briefly touch on it here (building on what was said in Chapter 14), then move on. It's included in our discussion because adopted kids almost always have been foster kids and thus have many of the same types of backgrounds, problems, and issues as foster kids. There's a truckload of pros and cons to consider in your decision about whether to foster or adopt. Both kinds of care require background checks, paperwork, references, training hours, and home inspections.

If you adopt, in a few months the child becomes yours alone. You have the same legal rights as with a biological child. You make all the decisions and take on all the burdens. You may or may not receive subsidy payments for the child's care.

If you foster, you have a support system for you and the child. But you also have someone looking over your shoulder, telling you what the child needs, as well as ongoing court dates for review of the case. Much more is provided for the *foster* child, such as clothing, free medical and dental care, free counseling and other mental health services, respite services, and ongoing support and training for you. You remain in a network of other foster parents, often attending social events and support group meetings with them. You may be required to get additional hours of training to retain your license. Of course, you, your home, and your child receive regular visits from a foster care worker. In addition, you always have someone to call in case of an emergency. But I've been told that in many large cities in particular caseworkers are so overloaded (and caseloads so large) that foster parents rarely see a social worker — and, in emergencies, usually end up calling on friends.

A large part of pre-service training involves evaluation. You are learning about the children and the system, and the licensing worker is learning about you. You are doing self-assessment, and the agency is assessing you. It isn't necessary to make major decisions at this time, but if at some point in the process you come to the conclusion that fostering and adopting are not for you, you should tell the social worker or trainer. It takes a great deal of time and effort to license a home, and resources are scarce!

In foster care, a child's biological family may play an important role in the child's life. Ideally foster and bio-families are included as part of a team, working together to solve problems that led to placement. Additional members of the team could include such individuals as the foster care worker, a counselor, a teacher, a probation officer, perhaps a doctor, and a daycare provider. Which people are on the team depends on the nature of the individual case. A set of goals will be formulated, and each team member participates in a different way to help reach those goals.

Of course, most situations are not ideal. But the bio-parents will still have an impact on the child. Visits will be set up, so as to maintain the relationship between parent and child. Parents may be required to change, in order to get their child back, and they may be resistant or angry. Foster parents may or may not have actual contact with bio-parents, but their children will show the effects of these visits.

Some children want to go back home, and some do not. In any case, anxiety tends to build before the visit, and the child's behavior may change. More often the behavior changes dramatically *after* home visits or visits conducted at the agency with supervision. Children may act up in school, not be able to sleep, become defiant, or exhibit anger. They may say things they heard from the parents or report things the parents did to them. They may criticize the foster parents or become depressed and weep. In our state, the law gives parents at least one hour of "parenting time" per week with their child. Young children are usually *required* to visit. Teens are not. I have seen many foster parents become friends with biological parents, who allow them to act as mentor or respite provider long after the placement has ended. If you attempt to develop a relationship of professional courtesy, respect, and trust, you can achieve much more for the child than if you have an adversarial relationship with your child's parents. On occasion friendship even develops. But beware of blurring boundaries or becoming an enabler for dysfunctional behaviors of the bio-parents!

Childcare providers

You must provide the licensing caseworker with the names and addresses of all persons other than you who may be caring for foster children from your home. This is so they can be checked out by your licensing agency and approved for spending time with your foster children. Usually this means that any daycare provider used must be licensed by the state.

When I was a single parent I discovered an interesting fact about daycare. In Michigan our local social services agency has a subsidized daycare program for low-income working parents of children 12 and under. This program is *required to pay for the care of foster children of any age!* Therefore, you can access a licensed daycare provider to supervise your foster teen while you're working, and it costs nothing. You can believe I passed this on to the working parents on my foster care caseload! These are the kinds of things experienced foster parents can share with newly licensed parents whom they mentor.

As touched on in Chapters 8 and 12, I recommend against using a foster child as a baby sitter. Why? Because these children and teens are often in the system because of poor parenting. Thus what model do they have to follow in parenting younger children? In addition, the number of children in the system who have been abused is astonishing, and why would they not abuse a younger child? Finally, if the child were able to care for himself or herself, why would they be placed with you? *You* are parenting them, and they should not parent others. In my years as a foster parent, I made this an ironclad rule.

The medical system

Foster and adopted children may have more interactions with a medical system than bio-children. Why? It is now acknowledged in most circles that stress frequently is a factor in the onset or worsening of physical illness. In addition, some children enter the system because of medical problems, such as addiction at birth or profound disabilities. Also, physical and emotional injuries result in medical intervention for abuse/neglect wards of the court. In most states an annual physical exam is required for foster children. Therefore, it's quite beneficial to have a family doctor who is willing to treat your foster children *and* who knows your family. The same is true of a therapist. Psychological and medical issues are intertwined, and your entire family is affected by the very fact that you foster or adopt a child into it. For many years my medical doctor has kept up on how many and what kind of children I had at home, as it had a bearing on the health of the whole family.

I should add that the psycho-emotional connection with physical problems will mean that you are a frequent visitor to the doctor's office with your foster/adopted special needs children. Since retiring from foster care, I have been amazed at how quickly my number of visits has dropped! Not only do the emotional problems cause illness, you also may be required to see a doctor for examination of a newly placed child who is a suspected abuse victim. Or you may have a hyperactive child who simply takes chances, runs a lot, rides fast on his/her bike, and gets more than the usual number of injuries from taking tumbles. With severely emotionally disturbed children or seriously depressed children, doctor visits or even hospital stays can stem from self-abuse or suicide attempts. For a few years I became a "regular" at our local emergency room because I often was needing to bring in such children as a result of frequent instances of self-abusive behavior.

Education

Foster and adoptive parents, like any parents, are encouraged to have a lot of interaction with the schools their children attend. It is the parents' job to advocate for the child — but also to support teachers and other school officials in matters of instruction and discipline. A defensive and angry parent helps no one, *and a poor example of problem solving is set for the child*.

A sizable number of foster children are behind their grade level in school. The many moves they make and the dysfunctional family system most have lived in both contribute to school failure. Therefore, foster parents may be spending much more time helping with schoolwork than they might with their bio-children. In addition, many foster children are categorized as "special education" students, so foster parents need to work with the special education department to implement plans for them.

It's of the utmost importance that foster parents understand the special education system and the rights of the child, the child's bio-parents, and the agency. If your child is in the special education system (categorized as learning disabled, emotionally impaired, developmentally disabled, or some other special designation), you should obtain a copy of the book on rights and responsibilities — and read it thoroughly. You will be attending individual educational planning conferences (IEPCs); a recent change in the special ed law allows foster parents to sign IEP forms. You will be asked about behaviors that you may observe or difficulties you see the child encounter. In general you should familiarize yourself with confidentiality rules, though you don't need to tell the school personnel every detail of the child's case. See Appendix F for a more in-depth discussion of confidentiality.

You should be familiar with the terms used in special education, such as DD (developmentally disabled), EI (emotionally impaired), EMI (educably mentally impaired), and so on. In addition, you should understand the "504 Rule" of the Americans with Disabilities Act and how it can help your child (the Americans with Disabilities Act, Rule 504, says schools and workplaces must accommodate persons with disabilities). Due to the limitations of space, see Appendix G for additional information about the "alphabet soup" of special education and related matters.

My favorite and most helpful reference on special education issues is Dr. Robert Anderson of Utah. He has made some cassette tapes that take you through a conference, give suggestions for things you or the school can do to help the child, and list rights you have (that even school officials may not know about).

Dr. Anderson suggests you take the *Special Education Rules & Laws* book to the meeting *and* a plan of what you would like the school to provide for your child. The best conference I ever attended was one for my biological son, who has ADHD and needed a "504 Plan." I brought copies of two things to hand out to all the conference attendees.

The first was a concise summary of my son's difficulties, along with references that described them, such as Hallowell and Ratey's

Driven to Distraction (showed I did my homework!). My synopsis included such observations as:

- "'Tom' has difficulty paying attention to the teacher, unless he can doodle while the teacher talks."
- "Tom has difficulty regaining control, once he begins to laugh or exhibit some other emotion, unless he can go into the hall where he is not observed for a minute."
- "Tom becomes bored when lessons become repetitive. He prefers to be allowed to work ahead and complete his homework assignment — or be allowed to do a special project."

The second part of my "handout" spelled out several suggestions that I hoped the school could adopt to assist my son — *and none of them would cost money or take additional personnel or time.* For example, he is now allowed to leave the room to "collect himself" if he gets overly emotional. If Tom feels he understands the lesson thoroughly, he is allowed to go to the back of the room and do assignments on a computer. He is allowed to doodle while the teacher lectures, without getting into trouble.

The school staff was grateful for the summary of ADHD behaviors, as well as my no-cost requests. After all, no teacher can know all the details of every impairment present in his/her classroom. Perhaps *you* are the expert on ADHD, Fetal Alcohol Syndrome, or Reactive Attachment Disorder. So it may be up to you to "educate the educators"!

Special education departments are hard-pressed to provide the services that are demanded of them. An increasing number of children are being "labeled" and sent to the special ed classes. *However, my study of Dr. Ruby Payne's theories has dramatically changed my opinion of these labels, and I now believe that many of our foster children are incorrectly labeled and placed. Differences in learning style, vocabulary, goals, and achievement standards make children raised in poverty often look like special education students to school personnel, as well as to the students' middle-class foster parents. A deeper understanding of these differences is vitally important. I am indebted to Dr. Payne for sharing the insights and materials of the next chapter.*

CHAPTER 16

Tips for Teaching and Relating

Contributed by Ruby K. Payne, Ph.D.

It isn't unusual for foster children to need assistance with academic skills. A disproportionate percentage of foster children come from a socioeconomic background of poverty or welfare.

In their research, Hart and Risley found the following with regard to language in 1- to 3-year-old children (in stable households by economic group):

Number of words heard	Economic group	Affirmations (strokes)	Prohibitions (discounts)
10 million words	Welfare	1 for every ...	2
20 million words	Working class	2 for every ...	1
30 million words	Professional	5 for every ...	1

Additionally, Martin Joos (1967), a Dutch linguist, found that every language in the world has five registers:

Register	Explanation
Frozen	Language that is always the same. For example: Lord's Prayer, wedding vows, etc.
Formal	The standard sentence syntax and word choice of work and school. Has complete sentences and specific word choice.
Consultative	Formal register when used in conversation. Discourse pattern not quite as direct as formal register.
Casual	Spoken language between friends and is characterized by a 400- to 800-word vocabulary. Word choice general and not specific. Conversation dependent upon non-verbal assists. Sentence syntax often incomplete.
Intimate	Language between lovers or twins. Language of sexual harassment.

In generational poverty (where the family or adult has been in poverty two generations or more), adults and children mostly know casual register. To do well in school and most jobs, one must be able to speak in the formal register. In fact, job interviews are a tool to find out if one can speak formal register.

Formal register is where the *abstract* words are. For example, we use a thermometer to measure temperature, but 40 degrees below zero can do much more damage to a body than 10 degrees below zero. Yet how the colder temperature *feels* to the body isn't much different from the 30-degree warmer one. Celsius or Fahrenheit references are *abstract representations* of temperature.

Other examples:

- A written score of music *represents* music but is not the music.
- A roadmap is an *abstract representation* of highways criss-crossing the countryside, a way of visualizing a concrete reality.

To survive in poverty, one must be highly non-verbal and sensory. Despite a high value on storytelling and entertainment in generational poverty, the most important information tends to be given non-verbally.

To survive in school and at work, one must be verbal and abstract. The important information is given verbally (both oral and written) and with a high degree of abstraction.

Therefore, for many foster children from generational poverty, the world of middle class is foreign, even alien. *Abstract referencing systems* are unfamiliar — such as maps, written documents, deeds, titles, checkbooks, savings accounts. *A written document (grades, report cards) has little or no value.*

Written documents can have value if it's explained that they are a medium of exchange. For example, you exchange a paycheck for cash. Grades are exchanged for jobs that pay more or for entrance into college.

The most effective way to help a child from poverty understand the abstract representational world is to use an analogy, a story, or a drawing (mental models). Just as a blueprint represents the house when finished, it also translates between the world of abstractions (word pictures) and the final three-dimensional object — the finished house.

An analogy that can be used to help children understand is to ask them if the TV guide is the same thing as a TV show. The guide represents the shows but is not the show.

How do you advocate for your foster child who was raised in poverty but must negotiate the middle-class hidden rules in your household and at school? Here are some tools and techniques.

Helping with reading

Reading involves two aspects — decoding and comprehension. Decoding means that you know the sound(s) a letter makes, and comprehension means that you can understand what you read. Many foster children can't even *get* to comprehension because they can't decode. There's a simple method to teach decoding. It uses signing developed by Dr. Bethanie H. Tucker called Tucker Signing Strategies. It's quick and inexpensive. For more information, call (800) 424-9484.

To teach comprehension, vocabulary is involved. The quickest way to teach vocabulary is to have students draw out the meaning of the word and take a playful approach to the word. A game that can be played involves the introduction of new words. The child makes up a meaning for a word that is new to him/her, then the real meaning/definition is discussed. The next day the child finds a word in the dictionary that you, the adult, aren't familiar with, and *you* make up a definition for it. Then the real meaning/definition is discussed.

Additionally, it's very important that you use the name of an object when referring to the object. For example, instead of saying, "Get that," the person would say, "Please pick the fork up from under the table."

Helping with math

Math is about assigning order and value to the universe. Without math we couldn't discuss distances or parts of a pizza. Math assigns value and order in three principal ways: time, space, or numbers. For example, fractions are about part-to-whole of space. Decimals are about part-to-whole of numbers. In order to do this, one must know right, left, front, back, top, bottom, etc. In poverty, most homes are so small that one can touch — or nearly touch — all the walls, so adverbs for space are seldom used.

Using graph paper where students must stay in the same column (color code the columns) helps tremendously. In addition, to rotate objects in space, students must have their eyes looking up because that is the neurological position that eyes are in when the brain is accessing visual information. Because so much of math has to do with space and the manipulation of spatial objects, it's important for them to move their eyes into that position.

In high school, successful completion of Algebra I is the course that best predicts whether a student will go to college. Successful completion of Algebra II in high school is the greatest predictor of whether a student will finish college or not. Both Algebra I and II are abstract representations of basic math. If a teenager struggles with algebra, it is usually worth the investment to hire a tutor.

Helping with imagination

Thinking in generational poverty tends to be in terms of polarities. In other words, options are seldom considered. For example: *"I like it. I hate it. It is good. It is bad."* Imagination is based in part on the ability to visualize options. That isn't so difficult unless emotions or oneself are involved. Then options are difficult. *One of the best ways to engage* imagination is to watch a TV show with the child and ask "What if" and "How might" questions.

- *What if he had never met that girl?*
- *What if he had not been lost?*
- *How might the ending have been different?*
- *How might his life have been different?*

Planning and goal setting

Vital to the success of the foster child and particularly the adolescent is the ability to **plan and set goals.** We teach this by teaching students to plan backward. In *The Seven Habits of Highly Effective People,* Stephen Covey says, "Begin with the end in mind." In other words, break down the task into parts, then ask, "How much time will you need each day to get this done?" For example, getting to school or work on time. What time to do you have to be there? Eight o'clock in the morning. OK, how long does it take you to get there? (Help them with this.) Add 10 minutes for emergencies. So, OK, you need to leave at 7:30 a.m. How long does it take you to get dressed? How many TV shows do you watch while you're getting dressed? OK, so you must get up at 6:30. How will you get up? Do you have an alarm clock?

This planning method also can be useful with the various steps needed to do school assignments, such as term papers or construction projects involving research. If it's a long assignment, use a calendar when going through this process with the student. The other method that works is to use 3-by-5 note cards. The students simply jot down a list of things they plan to get done that day. With school-age children, they answer two questions. "What is my plan for today" (academically and behaviorally)? Then at the end of the day they answer this question: "Did I do my plan? Why or why not?"

Time in generational poverty generally is kept emotionally, not abstractly. In other words, *time is how it feels.* Time is often kept according to what show is on TV.

Question making, code switching, and advocacy

One of the most valuable gifts you can give your foster child is to help him/her **learn to ask questions syntactically** (the logical sequencing of words based on the rules of grammar). This already was touched on above in "Helping with imagination." The kinds of questions presented there, when answered by the students, help them greatly in comprehension.

Another gift to your foster child is the concept of **code switching**. In other words, there are at least two sets of hidden rules: the rules that people follow in generational poverty help them survive there (for example, physical fighting and telling people off when they've crossed you in some way), but following those same rules is asking for trouble in middle class.

Too often the approach is to tell children in poverty that the hidden rules they know have no value, and the children "should know better." A better approach is to simply and directly say, "These are the rules here." Explain that their rules have value, but in this setting they don't help. *Use an analogy to playing a game. Do you use the same rules in football that you do in basketball?* Well, no. Why not? You would lose — or get kicked out of the game. Are you allowed to tackle in football? Yes. Are you allowed to tackle in basketball? No. *Different games, different rules.*

To advocate for the child in the school setting, it's important that you set up the following three-pronged approach to both academic and behavioral expectations *in writing:* the school/teacher will _____, the foster parents will _____, the foster child will _____. Then clearly outline in writing what the agreements are and what the approaches will be.

In advocating for the student at school, it's also useful to note that most teachers and administrators want to help the student. Especially for teenagers, it's important to talk to the teacher directly *while the foster child is there listening to the conversation.* If the foster child is going to be an equal player, he/she needs to be in on the conversation. To not have the student there only creates more distrust. However, careful judgment needs to be exercised when the student is in fifth grade or younger. Depending on the child and the subject matter, some meetings between teacher and foster parent are more productive without the youngster present. These should be decided on a case-by-case basis.

Another point in **advocating** for a foster child: It's better *not* to have a team approach — that is, six teachers and you and the student. This can be overwhelming to the student. Start with a teacher the foster child *likes* and ask for a conference before or after school. Get in writing what the requirements are and what must be done to pass the class. Have the child set a goal for passing; *a B is fine, and even a C is OK.*

Then you would have separate conferences with the other teachers whom the foster child does not like as well. (If the child has only one teacher and hates that teacher, find out if the child is justified in his/her feelings. If so, talk to the administrator about moving the child.)

At the beginning of each conference, simply say something like this: "I would like to tape record this conversation so that we can go back over it at home. We'd like to come up with a plan that will help us be successful. I'm not interested in dwelling on the negative but rather wish to find out what we need to do specifically to be successful here." No one wants to be recorded making unsubstantiated allegations and criticisms.)

If the teacher is rude or disrespectful to the student in the conference, or if the teacher gives negative, unsupported opinions about the foster child, ask the teacher, "Specifically, what data do you have to support your comments?" Feel free to remind the teacher that the purpose of the conference is *to solve problems and not assign blame* — that everyone is looking for the approaches and tools that will best help the child be successful. *The conference should end with a plan* for that to occur.

Teaching self-advocacy and coping skills: positive self-talk and procedural self-talk

In order to advocate for *oneself,* one must have **positive self-talk,** as well as **procedural self-talk.**

Most of us have *a little voice — positive self-talk —* inside our head that offers encouraging messages. These messages help us finish tasks, complete projects, and get through difficult situations. *Individuals from poverty often don't have this voice or, if they do, they have trouble hearing it.* (See chart at the start of this chapter regarding "Affirmations" and "Prohibitions" for children growing up in welfare situations.) When this positive voice is not heard, the success rate is much lower.

Procedural self-talk is the voice that talks an individual through a task. It's a key to success. Many individuals in poverty have a very limited support system — and particularly missing is procedural self-talk. Many tasks are started but never finished. In numerous dealings with students from poverty, teachers and other school officials find that self-talk is simply not available.

Voices

One of the biggest issues with foster children from poverty is the fact that many such children have had to function as their own parents. *They have parented themselves and others — often younger siblings. In many instances they also have acted as parent to the adult in the household.* (See the references in Chapters 2 and 3 to "parentified children.")

Inside virtually everyone's head are three internal **voices** that guide the individual. These voices are the **child voice**, the **parent voice**, and the **adult voice**. It would appear that individuals who became their own parent quite young don't have an internal adult voice. They have a child voice and a parent voice but not much of an adult voice. Not only do parentified children struggle with this, it's also true for me and, I daresay, quite a few other foster parents as well. We need to strengthen our adult voice!

An internal adult voice allows for "give and take." This voice provides the language of negotiation and allows issues to be examined in a non-threatening way.

Voices

Child

- *Quit picking on me.*
- *You don't love me.*
- *You want me to leave.*
- *Nobody likes (loves) me.*
- *I hate you.*
- *You're ugly.*
- *You make me sick.*
- *It's your fault.*
- *Don't blame me.*
- *He/she did it.*
- *You make me mad.*

Parent

- *You (shouldn't) should do that.*
- *It's wrong (right) to …*
- *That's stupid, immature, out of line, ridiculous.*
- *Life's not fair. Get busy.*
- *You are good, bad, worthless, beautiful (any judgmental, evaluative comment).*
- *You do as I say.*
- *If you weren't so …, this wouldn't happen to you.*

Adult

- *I need …*
- *What's your plan?*
- *What are choices in this situation?*
- *If you choose …, then you have chosen …*
- *If you did know, what would you say?*
- *When you did that, what did you want?*
- *How did that behavior help you be successful?*

It's important that you and your children become able to use the adult voice. The adult voice is non-judgmental, free of negative non-verbal, factual, often in a question format, and has an attitude of win/win.

Build resiliency skills

Here are some questions to ask your children that will help build resiliency.

Insight	Why?
Independence	How am I different?
	How is this situation not about me?
Relationships	With whom do I have mutual respect?
Initiative	What can I do?
	What parts can I address?
Creativity	What is your purpose?
	What are the rules here?
Humor	What about this is funny?
Morality	What is the right thing to do?
	What is humane, kind, compassionate?
	What is the least destructive way to handle it?

By using these tips for teaching and relating, foster and adoptive parents and their children should be better able to enjoy each others' company — *and* withstand the scrutiny that often comes with the territory. Welcome to the glass house!

CHAPTER 17

Living in a Glass House

We now come to a discussion of the impact of fostering on *and within* the community. It behooves foster parents to keep themselves alert to the reactions of friends and family. In some cases the parents are looked upon with admiration and strongly supported by friends and family. In others, however, they are criticized and ostracized because they have "those kinds of kids" in their home. My husband and I have experienced both, and we're now more sensitive to reactions.

In many ways a foster family lives in "a glass house." Privacy is greatly reduced, judgments are made, and tales are told.

- First, the agency inspects the house, looking for safety issues or health issues.

- Second, personal references are required and, in my case, the licenser called the references and had a nice long talk with them. The main purpose of such calls is to establish that the foster parents are "of good character."

- Third, children placed in your home talk about things that go on in their daily life, which means many children at school or in the neighborhood hear things. What they hear may or may not be accurate. For example, a recent foster child told me he thought we were very rich. Of course, his perspective came from his own family's circumstances, and they live in a poor neighborhood with very little income. And he believed we were paid extremely well for keeping him, although we never told him how much we received.

- Fourth (related to the previous point), we never told any child how much we received for their care, because we never wanted them to compare notes with each other. In this way, we avoided issues like "That's *my* money, and I want it," or "Ha! I'm worth more than you are," or "I deserve more toys than you — because they get paid more for me."

Children also would talk about what they'd hear and see in our home. If one of us would lose our temper or make a mistake, the foster children felt free to talk about it at school. If one of us had a problem with drugs or alcohol, it wouldn't have taken much to cause a child to "tell" on us to authorities.

If licensers receive any complaints, they must investigate very thoroughly to see if the home is a danger to children placed there. This can be uncomfortable for all concerned. The allegations are presented to the foster family. At that point a thorough investigation is conducted, with children being questioned, neighbors and friends being asked, and the observations of the social worker recorded. Until the family in question is cleared, the agency usually puts a "hold" on placements in that home.

Neighbors also judge and comment on the foster family. The children placed in the home judge and comment to the foster parents, friends, and their own bio-families. For example, it's quite common for foster children to declare that the bio-children in the home don't have to do anything, while the foster children have to do all the work. Or they might comment on a foster parent whose language is inappropriate, such as swearing. Or they may tell you your home isn't clean and that "you're a slob." If you don't have (or *develop*) thick skin, these comments may hurt or bother you a great deal.

Also remember, a child coming into your home may have so little sense of appropriate boundaries that he/she feels free to search drawers and closets, open doors to bedrooms, and generally invade private areas. This is quite common.

If you aren't able to tolerate this "fishbowl" openness and "display" of your home, think carefully before getting a license. In addition, foster children have little if any personal investment in you or your things, so they may tell friends and other outsiders exactly what goes on in the family. (In extreme cases they might even report to a teenage peer where your valuables are kept.) Of course, older bio-children frequently criticize the way a parent is doing things too, so such feedback tends to come with the territory when teens are involved. But with foster children, the feeling of being exposed to the community tends to increase substantially.

CHAPTER 18

Long-Term Support for the Child *and* You

Suppose you have adopted a child and, four or five years later, the child begins to have very serious problems with the school or legal system. Is help available?

* * *

While doing social work in a crisis intervention program, I sometimes got calls from adoptive parents many years after the adoption was final. They were having problems when their child reached puberty and after — and didn't have any idea how to cope.

At that point should the parents **expect** support because their child is adopted? Or should things be exactly the same as for parents of a biological child? This is certainly an ethical dilemma for an adoption agency and a matter of considerable debate among service providers. Questions include:

- Is the agency that arranged the adoption many years before still responsible to support the parents?
- If the adoption agency is also a foster care agency (quite common), should the foster care staff attempt to intervene in the crisis?

- If the child had a therapist (psychologist, psychiatrist, mental health provider), is it that person's responsibility to assist in follow-up of their client?
- Or should the parents simply have to tough it out like the parents of biological children, and find whatever help would be available to them?

Only recently have adoption agencies in my state begun providing services to such families. It's my belief that this goes hand in hand with the strong push at the state level to find homes for special needs children. The last few years our state officials (in Michigan) have revised foster care and adoption laws, have done extensive studies of children in the system, and have attempted to find a way to provide a home for *every* homeless child in the system. This means they're placing children with more severe difficulties and handicaps than ever before. And many of these children are extremely difficult to parent. Therefore, in order to avoid hundreds of broken adoptions, it became necessary to provide extra support.

To begin with, a family with an adopted child should be able to access any type of support the family of bio-children can access. But, in addition, if the special needs of the adopted child have been documented, they should be able to obtain help from any number of agencies and sources tailored to the specific needs of that child. They also should be able to get assistance with paying for the services through their adopted child's medical subsidy. (Ah, the importance of putting that in place *before* finalizing the adoption!)

Why do we even need to discuss this problem? Do adopted children present any bigger challenge than other teens? The answer is "yes." Remember the discussions earlier about attachment problems, nurture needs, abuse, trauma, abandonment, and other problems? Many of these don't manifest themselves until the child reaches puberty. At that point the parents face far more serious problems than the parents of bio-children. Whether or not the agency is required to help them is the controversial question, but it's clear they *do* need help if their child begins to act out in his/her teens!

This recently hit home for our family when one of our adopted children committed a serious crime. My husband and I were quite worried about the expense of foster care or residential placement. We also wanted to know if we should consider breaking the adoption, if he should come home, if he needed a lawyer, and other considerations. Even with all our experience in adopting and fostering, we weren't sure where to turn. I reasoned that the folks at the adoption agency had a stake in keeping the adoption permanent, so how could they advise us objectively? I knew that the boy's therapist was committed to maintaining an intact family for the child. I knew that my medical doctor wanted us to break the adoption and stop fostering, due to the state of my physical and emotional health. So whom could I ask?

This is when a support group is crucial. My "system" friends were there for me. And when I finally went to the adoption worker, she told me she could assist our family in obtaining funding through our adoption subsidy, *if* the child were court-ordered into placement. In addition, our therapist asked that I come in for several weeks to deal with the stress and issues related to keeping or breaking the adoption. My doctor reviewed the situation with me and with other family members. These are some examples of how one's support system can help you, as well as some of the questions that adoptive parents face that others may not.

Yes, special needs children can have more severe problems, and they do need more support, but some agencies and states in the U.S. haven't yet put these supports into place. Some common programs are family camps for adoptive families, support group meetings for adoptive or foster parents, special social events for foster and adoptive families, and training classes designed to assist parents in understanding special needs. If your community doesn't provide adequate support, perhaps you should initiate it or lobby for it. Learn about programs that others offer — in order to have a model to emulate. Seek a mentor, or offer to mentor someone else.

Above all, keep your faith strong, and trust in God to help you because you are helping God's children. As a Christian, I draw great comfort from the words of Jesus in the 25th chapter of the Gospel of Matthew, verse 40:

"Whatever you did for the least of these ... you did for me."

CHAPTER 19

Pitfalls

After parenting other people's children for 20 years, I have come to recognize a number of pitfalls along the road of this great adventure. Here are four.

* * *

'All you need is love'

By this time in our discussion, I trust you understand that you need a lot more than love to care for some of the children you are parenting. "All you need is love" may once have been true for these children, but they didn't get it, so now they — and others — must pay the price.

In some cases, you may need to become a "professional parent," with a great deal of knowledge, experience, objectivity, and strength. In others, nurturing will be the most important thing you give. And with older children, besides everything else, you would be doing well to give them independent-living skills to use when they finally leave your family and the "system."

'I can mold this child'

Have you learned by now that this statement is probably false? In fact, isn't it false even if it's your biological child? Why?

- Conception factors: genes, health/disease, addiction.
- Pre-natal issues: health/disease, mental state of the mother, substance abuse, nutrition, mother's environment.
- First moments, days, and months (you'll notice I didn't say *years*) of the child's life outside the womb. An overwhelming number of factors now enter in and have a major effect on the new life that is forming.

If you make the statement, "I wanted an infant, but I'll take a child under 3 because *I can still mold and shape the child the way I want him/her to be,*" you may need to reread portions of this book! And never lose sight of the fact that puberty brings with it a whole new bag of problems. It seems the rush of hormones and the usual adolescent confusion are compounded many times over in these children, and their adolescence can be stormy indeed. I've seen lovely little children turn into monsters when their hormones started surging. There are times — usually around puberty — when issues begin to surface that the child never even knew existed. In the words of the Boy Scout motto, be prepared!

It also ought to be clear by now that babies and toddlers already have much of their personalities formed *before* they come into your family. Genes play one part, maternal health another, and environment a third. While it's true that parents can teach a child and that psychotherapy, along with a good healthy environment for many years, can have a great deal of positive impact on a child, it's *not* true that parents can make (or remake) a child "in their image." The opportunity to achieve change and adaptation is greater with a younger child, but some damage is so severe that parents have very little chance to undo more than a fraction of that damage.

Different parents find different things difficult to live with. I for one can't/won't keep a child with fetal alcohol syndrome, but I'd welcome a blind or deaf child. While I thrive on working with teenagers, I don't handle babies very well. For example, I couldn't stand getting up in the night, the total dependency, and the restricted movement that an infant would cause for me.

In sum, keep the following five factors in mind:

1. When placing a child in foster care, appropriate relatives are sought first. (Why isn't this child with them?)
2. Many factors affect infants, even in the uterus.
3. Environmental factors have tremendous impact during the first year of life.
4. Virtually all children who don't live with their biological parents feel the loss and grieve it.
5. Many psycho-emotional problems don't become evident in children until puberty.

Being an 'enabler'

By taking another person's child into your heart and home, we see that you are a helper and caretaker. However, do your best *not* to be an enabler for a child's or family's pathology. Do not support inadequate parenting, inadequate performance, or inadequate discipline. If things turn inside out and you become dependent on the child for your happiness — and foster due to your own deep personal needs — you are dangerously close to reinforcing three things: negative behaviors, substance abuse, and other equally dysfunctional actions. Be an "abler" (not an "enabler") and provide something for your child and his/her family that they've never had before: unconditional love with no strings attached.

'Friends and family will understand and support me'

Many families and friends do support people who decide to foster or adopt. However, just as many do not. In my case, my parents and siblings believe that the foster children take away something from my own children, utilize my resources that were meant for my family, and do damage emotionally to all of us in the bio-family. Neither my parents nor my husband's siblings recognize our adopted children as part of our immediate family *or* our family's descendants. However, friends of my husband and me strongly support us in our vocation/ministry and have been wonderful resources for us.

In addition, your social life could be curtailed if you choose to take a child with intensive needs, just as when a couple has a new baby. And if you have a child (or children) who might steal or damage property, you wouldn't want to take them to your friends' homes.

Finally, how many friends or family members do you have who could accommodate a half-dozen or so children from a group foster home ... if you would like to go for a visit?

To be sure, each situation is different, and each family is too. Only you will know whether you can count on support from family and friends. And you may not know for certain how people close to you will feel about fostering and/or adopting until you actually take the plunge. But don't simply expect that support; you may be in for a surprise!

CHAPTER 20

Parenting Your Grandchildren

You've looked forward to your retirement years to slow down, enjoy some of the things you sacrificed for your children while raising them, take up a few hobbies, or perhaps do some traveling. Instead, however, you find yourself starting over! The "pitter-patter of little feet" now greets your ears in the morning, and the old familiar morning rush to catch the school bus is once again your routine.

* * *

Grandparents who are raising their grandchildren are becoming more and more common in U.S. society. There are multiple reasons for this. To name just a few:

- An increase of drug and alcohol addiction.
- An increase of Child Protective Services involvement in each of our lives.
- A growing number of single teenage mothers bringing their babies to their parental home because it's increasingly accepted in their communities.
- A rising divorce rate, coupled with the rise in cost of living, which makes it difficult for single young mothers to survive on their own while raising babies.
- The death of one or both parents (sometimes from AIDS).

It's difficult to imagine and write about all the possible situations and circumstances where you raise someone else's child. It may be that the following discussion about raising your grandchildren also pertains to raising your nieces and nephews, raising your younger siblings, raising your best friend's child, and more.

Raising your grandchildren presents a whole new set of challenges to meet, along with a major shift in perspective and goals during your later years. To be sure, there are many rewards and joys in having young children around again, and if you asked those of us who are doing it, we wouldn't give it up for the world!

You might ask, Just what is different about it? Well, I can answer from my own experience — twice! I had my first two children when I was 18 and 20, then my last three when I was 38, 39, and 41. The gap between them was nearly the same as if the second set had been my grandchildren. In addition, I am currently parenting the child of one of my adopted children, yet *another* generation later.

The biggest difficulty most grandparents have to face is their relationship with their own children — the parent(s) of the child they are raising. Young mothers who bring their baby to their parental home while they're still attending high school often want help with the work, but they still want control of their own child. This can result in daily conflict over the simplest of things, such as how often to bathe a newborn, how many blankets to wrap the baby in, eating and sleeping schedules, discipline, food, or any aspect of life in which the baby plays a part. Mothers who aren't living with the grandparents may have been forced to give up their children due to addiction, neglect/abuse issues, or other factors that can mean they're angry and hurt and don't *want* their parents raising their children.

No matter what the reasons, the situation is a surefire formula for differences of opinion and trouble! It can be very difficult to have to choose between your child and your grandchild. And if conflicts become volatile or even violent, you just may have to make that choice.

As mentioned elsewhere in this book, many of the older children who enter the foster care or adoption system don't have enough skills or knowledge for independent living. When you adopt a child of 15 to 17, about all you can do is put a safety net under them and hope they'll come to you if they get into trouble, so you can steer them back to the road. Therefore, if your older children become a parent, you may find yourself doing quite a bit of their parenting for them. Now you have "adopted *grand*children"! (I prefer to call ours the "bonus" we got when we adopted her mom.)

One difference in raising children again is your energy level. It is difficult to keep up with a toddler. It's hard to get up during the night for infants. It is even *painful* to get down on the floor to play, if you have arthritis like I do!

What do you like to do? Is it the same as what you liked to do 20 or 30 years ago? I find, in my 50s, that I don't really enjoy the kindergarten Christmas pageant, the all-school field day, taking youngsters Trick or Treating, or listening to the first painful year of instrumental music in the school band. I'm tired of being a room mother, band booster, baby-sitter, and fund-raiser. Don't get me wrong. All those things are fun, once in a while, in the appropriate grandmother role. But when you become obligated on a long-term basis, the second time around can get to be a drag!

I can remember my son (in the second batch of kids) saying to me at the sledding hill, "Mom, how come the other moms ride the saucers down the hill with their kids, and you just sit in the car and crochet afghans?" Oops! (Well, at least I made the costumes for all the kindergartners doing the Easter play.)

But it's not all hardship and difficulty, and the rewards far outweigh the work — because a bright smile, dancing feet, and sparkling eyes certainly *do* brighten up our day and liven up our house again. After dealing with a house full of teens for a few years, our little "angel" is quite refreshing. And my husband is fond of telling her that her job here is to "make Grandma smile." She takes him very seriously, and I find myself laughing a lot more these days!

When you're older, you usually have more financial resources than you did in your 20s, and can buy some really nice things for your grandchild. For example, we are sending ours to a parochial school, which we couldn't afford for our children years ago.

Having a "companion in the kitchen" who chatters happily while we do dishes, make cookies, or wash windows certainly makes those jobs more fun. Having the time and experience to make her a very special

Easter dress this year was great too. And it turned out to be just beautiful!

In many cases, Grandma has the help of her own children to baby sit, entertain, and generally assist with the parenting. There are days when I'm extremely grateful to my 15- or 16-year-old for taking my granddaughter along to visit friends. I catch a quick nap and wake up ready for more fun!

One retired couple I know may be typical of many couples today. With the high rate of divorce in America, your husband may not be the biological grandparent of the child you are raising. You may have divorced and remarried — and now your young adult son is in trouble. You can't abandon him, and your new husband gets to help you with a child that is no part of him. Whoosh! There go the retirement years he expected to spend peacefully with you. Sound like fertile ground in which to grow resentment? You bet!

If you have your grandchildren because their parents are addicted to drugs or alcohol, you also might have gotten kids with such problems as fetal alcohol syndrome or infant drug addiction. Therefore, these children may be quite difficult to raise.

My husband and I are more than delighted to be raising our beautiful little granddaughter. We find it far more rewarding than difficult. We are glad we made the choice to do it.

Legal issues

Before taking this step, my husband and I received some very good advice. We were told to get a **legal guardianship** and not just take the child in. Although we didn't know it at the time, we were establishing our legal authority to make decisions regarding our granddaughter, obtain medical care, register her in school, and keep her with us until our daughter can stabilize her own life. We were preventing our granddaughter from being moved back and forth at her mother's whim and ensuring that her mother is completely able to parent her before she takes her daughter back home.

There are many types of authority the court can grant parents or grandparents over the life of a child. What we have is called a

voluntary temporary guardianship. This means that her mother voluntarily relinquished her parental rights and stipulated what she would do in order to get her child back. We filed to take guardianship, filled out a form, and the court scheduled a guardianship hearing. Our daughter stated the reason she was willing to let our granddaughter come to stay with us, then checked boxes on the form, which listed specific things. A few of them were:

- Obtain appropriate housing to provide for herself and her children.
- Become self-supporting by obtaining and maintaining a job.
- Provide medical insurance for her children.
- Maintain her relationship with her child by having regular and frequent visits with her while she lives with us.
- Provide financial support for her.

After she has done those things, she can file a petition to dissolve guardianship, and the court will decide if a change is appropriate at that time. This might be the kind of guardianship to use in the case of spouse abuse, long-term hospitalization of a parent, temporary difficulties of a serious enough nature to need a different home for the children, or even parental abuse that could be corrected with appropriate services provided for the parent(s).

Another kind of arrangement is a **permanent guardianship.** This is more appropriate in a case where parental rights are actually terminated by the court, and the court awards custody to the grandparents. It would not be reversible. It could be granted if a parent goes to prison for a relatively long time (determined by the state you live in). In Michigan it's defined as two years or more.

Yet a third kind is **legal adoption.** It could occur in the above case, in the case of the death of your child and spouse (leaving your grandchildren orphans), in the case of permanent disability of your child, or in any case where there's never going to be any way for your grandchildren to be raised by their biological parents.

Of course, informal arrangements between families occur all the time. You don't *have* to involve the court. The only thing you have to consider is your *legal right to obtain medical care or register the grandchildren in school — or sign documents for them.* If there's no legal guardianship or adoption, their parents must do all that.

Grandparents also can *partially* raise their grandchildren, such as in the case of being **daycare providers.** The parents may both be working and ask the grandparents to be daycare providers for them. If the grandparents are willing and able, how wonderful it is for their grandchildren! No strangers baby sitting. No expensive daycare centers. No danger of disease or injury from other children. In most cases like this, the grandchildren will not have "special needs" caused by their parents' problems or genetic ones. They will not be emotionally impaired due to neglect or abuse. The main problems that may arise are such matters as differing opinions among the parents and grandparents on discipline or other areas of child rearing. And these problems can occur with *anyone* who parents someone's child, related or not!

Financial issues

Some grandparents are able to collect Social Security, veterans' benefits, or retirement money while raising their grandchildren. Some receive support from the children's parents, either voluntary or court-ordered. Some may even be able to collect welfare or obtain state-sponsored insurance, if they're unable to provide it themselves. However, before the state is willing to support the children, it always will see if the child's parents can do so.

In the case of permanent legal custody, such as permanent guardianship or adoption, grandparents would do well to consider what will happen to the grandchildren if they die before the grandchildren turn 18. Depending on the health and age of the grandparents, this could be a very important consideration. (To be sure, all parents must think about this, but the possibility of untimely death is much greater, of course, if the grandparents are elderly.)

Another consideration is one or both grandparents becoming invalid(s), requiring the grandchildren to care for *them,* instead of the other way around. One more possibility to ponder!

Looking beyond today

Sometimes I wonder how I will like dealing with a teenager when I am in my 60s and my husband is in his 70s! Will we be so out of touch that we "don't have a clue" what is going on? Or will be just as knowledgeable as any parent, because we have been doing this all along, and our granddaughter actually keeps us in touch? How will we cope with driver education? With dating? With puberty, rebellion, defiance, school dances, class rings? Even as our current teenagers go through these things, we find we are quite old-fashioned in our beliefs, and we struggle with some of today's normal teenage behaviors. How much *more* difficult will it be in 10 years?

Foster Cline and Jim Fay (the creators of "Love and Logic," noted in Chapter 10) have written a book called *Parenting Your Grandchildren*. In it they address a wide array of issues and have some great suggestions for us grandparents who are "starting all over."

The biggest problem for my husband and me was solved when we took action to make our guardianship legal. Now we're dealing with our relationship with our adopted daughter. But any discussion of parenting grandchildren always includes the joys and fun times the grandparents have, as well as the focus and direction it has given them.

The moment my husband returns from work, our granddaughter runs to greet him and give him a hug. Just seeing his face light up makes it all worthwhile right there. And, as noted earlier, our darling granddaughter makes *me* smile too.

There are probably many things I haven't thought of, but I'm sure we'll be able to cross those bridges as we have the ones behind us — with faith in God and ourselves, along with the wisdom and experience of age *and* the children with whom we've already gone through the great adventure!

CHAPTER 21

Fostering or Adopting Babies and Toddlers

What makes you any better than their parents?

It is my hope that, after gaining an understanding of the differences in parenting styles, lifestyles, class structure, and circumstances of life, you will begin to see you are not *better at* parenting, only *different from* the biological parents in the system. It's unfortunate that the courts and welfare system are both operating under the standards designed by the middle class. Why do I say unfortunate? Because usually they're dealing with, and are intending to help, the segment of Americans who live in poverty. "Good!" you say. They need the help, don't they? Many do, indeed, need assistance, but in a different way.

The standards that many low-income parents must meet in order to prove to the court that they aren't neglectful or abusive are seldom designed with an understanding of the lifestyle and barriers the poor must cope with. They also don't reflect the different class standards and learning styles of generational poverty. Worse, these standards in effect condemn an entire way of life. Therefore, many children are removed from their home because their parents were unable to meet the standards set for them. They are then placed with parents who may have expectations these children cannot meet — and the children subsequently fail in school, in their social life, and (indeed) with their foster parents.

Have you ever wondered why so few wealthy people are foster parents? (This was addressed in greater detail in Chapter 8.) Or why so few non-white homes are available? I believe that the wealthy have standards and expectations the children cannot possibly meet (and don't even *want to try* to meet!), while many non-white families have standards and customs that are unacceptable to the middle-class licensing workers.

But we're talking about babies and toddlers, aren't we?! Well, as you have seen, babies already are affected by the time they are born. If they have been exposed to drugs or alcohol, if they're deformed or medically fragile, they may not "fit" into the homes of the wealthy. If you get a toddler, that child already has begun to form a value system very different from middle-class expectations; the subtle differences may not be apparent at first glance. However, language formation, defense mechanisms, eating habits, lines of authority, and many more things are already being programmed into their brain, and moving them will necessitate a whole new way of living life.

The work of Dr. Ruby Payne has opened the eyes of many teachers and school administrators. It is my hope that foster and adoptive parents can benefit from this work as well, along with social workers and court personnel who deal with the entire range of people's class backgrounds — and currently aren't known for considering that criterion when matching up families.

Dr. Payne and I, of course, do not condone neglect and abuse. However, there are many standards set for parents that have little to do with abuse. Parents are asked to appear in court and at the welfare agency during hours that may prevent them from going to work. Or they may have no adequate transportation or childcare. They may be required to follow detailed case plans — which call for extensive reading, writing, and recordkeeping skills — and live up to standards impossible for them. For example, many women living in poverty are single parents. The court frowns on cohabitation, yet people who live in poverty often don't marry, or they have a common-law relationship. The court expects parents to pay fines and costs for their children, yet they're often living on subsistence wages that leaves nothing extra for such expenses.

There are many other examples, but this book is not intended to explain all such differences in standards. Its main intent is to help you parent these children.

Ideally you will be stable, informed, and "of good character." However, that doesn't necessarily mean you are "better" than their parents who *may not be able* to care for their children. They may have very little money, poor health, no support system, illness, or other circumstances that prevent them from raising their own children, even though they love them. When you bring these children into your home, you attempt to help them in school and teach them middle-class values about money, marriage, respect for authority, and so on. And even though they may be very young, these children can see quite clearly that you are not like them.

Often even very young children have been taught to fear authority figures, to lie to "the establishment," and to fight fiercely to keep the family together. This is because relationships are so important to these families. They may have nothing else! It's imperative that you teach with understanding and compassion and not criticize or cut down their parents. Young children in particular usually want to please and are quick learners, but they may not want to call you "Mom" or "Dad" or embrace your attempts to nurture.

On the positive side in a home where there has been multi-generational poverty, very young children often have learned to be self-sufficient (as also noted in Chapter 16 in the "Voices" section). They have helped care for the younger children, fended for themselves in their parents' absence, and know much more than you might suspect.

In fact, they may be far more alert to danger than your bio-children because they didn't always have a hovering parent around to protect them. This is an example of learned survival behavior that is frequently misinterpreted by school personnel or parents. These children are alert, not "distracted." They are processing bits of information about their environment, not "missing the lesson." They are dealing with loss and grief, not "daydreaming." And they have developed learning styles different from your bio-children. They aren't necessarily special education students. But, since they're often far behind in their academics, they're frequently placed in special education categories and placed in special education classrooms. It's time American educators and parents took another look at these diagnoses, with a new understanding of what is "normal."

This information isn't meant to discourage. It's meant to help parents better understand and meet the needs of the children they're raising — and to assist social workers in matching children with families.

The trauma of separation and the inability to understand

The children who come into your home as babies and toddlers suffer the same trauma and loss as older children. They usually have no way of understanding their feelings or circumstances, however, and precious few coping mechanisms. It's your duty to help them through the grieving process, give them hope and nurture, and reassure them that they can depend on you for protection and safety. Always remember that their sense of time and future are much different from yours — and their vision much narrower. Be there for them!

I think the biggest pitfall for parents of these children is the failure to recognize that they have been affected, even in infancy, by the losses and, in some cases, dysfunction of their parents. Not all the effects show up in infancy.

One of the children who came to live in my home had an unusual knowledge of sexual matters for a 4-year-old. No one could get her to discuss any sort of sexual abuse or inappropriate behavior by adults toward her, but she clearly had knowledge no 4-year-old should have. There can be several explanations for this that don't indicate that this child was actually assaulted or raped. One is that she was exposed to sexual activity or pornography when she was very young, even before she developed language. If so, she would have no frame of reference in which to describe it or talk about it. A related possibility is that she heard things she didn't understand, such as the sounds of adults having sex. The girl exhibited all the symptoms of a sexually abused child, but she could tell no one — at least in any kind of understandable way — that she was.

In another instance (in my role as a foster care caseworker), I had placed four young boys in a foster home, and the very experienced foster parent called me the second day, requesting that I split them up. She said they frequently "acted out" the sex act, as well as actually performing some acts with each other. When we did split up the sibling group, the friends and neighbors of the foster parents were angry, saying that was unfair to the children. Of course, they didn't know the reason for the split! And two of the boys went to an equally experienced set of parents who had coped with this type of behavior before. The two foster homes worked with me to maintain the ties between the brothers, conducting visits at least twice a week, baby sitting for each other, and doing "parent therapy" with the boys in order to eliminate the behaviors. Eventually parental rights were terminated, and all four boys were adopted together, although we moved them in two at a time.

Very young children shouldn't know about things of a sexual nature, and all parents should be alert for signs of that or of physical abuse, reporting it immediately to their caseworker or the police.

Some foster parents find, after a year or two, that the toddlers they're caring for aren't developing as they should. Perhaps they're autistic or have been affected by alcohol or drugs. Perhaps they've been "failure-to-thrive" babies, suffering physical and emotional deprivations that are extremely difficult to change.

Warning: If you choose to foster these youngsters, be prepared for a broken heart! The courts do their level best to reunite families. Objectively one can understand where judges are coming from, but it doesn't make being a foster parent (who has grown attached to a child) any easier. There will be visits to the bio-parents' home(s), despite the fact that many of the young children beg not to go. There will be long separations from their families, then visits, and the heartache of separation all over again. And no matter how the foster parents view the biological family, the children almost always are reunited with that family, and the foster parents are the ones who are left crying!

If the child has an attachment disorder, you may have a youngster who isn't responsive to any of your attempts to bond or love. You can gaze into those beautiful eyes, smile and coo at the tiny face, and no reaction or response is forthcoming. If you're the kind of person who can parent that type of child, my hat is off to you! For me, as I mentioned earlier, there must be both give and take — and some kind of response to my overtures of kindness and love. Otherwise, I tend to view the child more as a job or duty. I am less eager to stand up and advocate for such children, I have less feeling for our relationship, and I've found (to my consternation) that in general I tend to make less effort on the child's behalf.

Despite my admittedly inconsistent track record as a foster parent, I like to think the children who have passed through my home have seen and learned many things they might not have learned otherwise. I have wanted to broaden their horizons, so to speak, and show them a world of opportunity, then teach them how to go out and seize it! Here are some specifics of what I've tried to do in my years of parenting other people's children, as well as my own (have fun coming up with your own list):

- I took my kids on vacations designed, at least in part, to teach.
- I allowed them to make mistakes, through which they learned.
- I exposed them to new foods, fads, languages, and ways of behaving.
- I took them to church, nice restaurants, and friends' homes.
- We went on field trips to museums, libraries, and farms.
- They could take music lessons, have pets, and help cook.
- My kids learned how to clean a room, budget their allowance, and choose their wardrobe.
- They learned to shop, make decisions, and relate to strangers.
- I asked them to dress appropriately for the occasion; I observe them behaving in social situations that I could monitor.
- Some needed help learning to do homework, while others needed lessons in bathing!
- I've taught them how and when to call 9-1-1, including what information to give the operator. (There's a sample page in Appendix D that should be hung near every phone in a foster home.)

Virtually *everything* we've done at our house has been a lesson in life. And I've tried to keep the primary goal of parenting in focus: preparing them to *leave me.*

> The goal of good parenting is to prepare your child to leave you. Giving a child survival skills and skills for independent living is one of the best gifts a parent can give a child. Being there for children when they need you — and standing back to let them learn from their mistakes — is the twofold goal of child rearing. Then, as they move into their teens, gradually give them their freedom.

Let's now move from younger children to older children. Since all of parenting is a process of learning to let go, let's *go* to the subject of fostering and adopting older children, the ones who are closest to spreading their wings and attempting to fly.

CHAPTER 22

Fostering or Adopting Older Children

*"There are only two lasting bequests
parents give their children:
roots and wings."*
-Author Unknown

The older-child adoption or the older foster child — and their need for practical skills for independent living

The closer children are to becoming an adult, the more necessary it is to give them the skills to survive in a difficult world. Your ability to assess and fulfill their needs will allow them to leave the system and become happy and productive members of society.

Appendix B in this book lists several things you can do to help your teenage children gain independence. Some of these ideas are things you can do *for* them — and others *with* them. You likely will be able to think of many more as you observe the teens coming into your foster home.

It almost goes without saying that older children come with "baggage," and you will need to accept it with them. Understand that *you* may not be able to change some things and that your job is to provide them with the knowledge that will allow *them* to *make choices* about what kind of life they will need. See the "roots and wings" quote at the outset of this chapter!

Helping them to learn practical skills is only part of it. You'll also be providing support, nurture, encouragement, and modeling, as well as the knowledge that you'll be there long after they move out. We have adopted four teenage children and accepted guardianship of our 5-year-old granddaughter (child of one of the four teenagers). Bud and I don't necessarily count all four adoptions as "success stories," but we hope we've given the children some sense of choice and a picture of how life could be for them.

Social skills and traditions are among the most difficult to teach. This is because your customs and traditions and behaviors are integrally tied to your social class and heritage. It may be an area that older children resist because they don't see these as something you *learn*. Or it may seem to them that you're trying to foist *your* values onto them. Further, you may be trying to teach them at an emotion-filled time in your or their life.

For example, not long ago we had a death in our family. My mother died. It happened that our home was the "gathering place" for family members and the "bed and breakfast" for the out-of-towners. All of my children needed to be taught the customs associated with this emotional event. While we know that funeral customs vary from culture to culture and religion to religion, there are some generally accepted behaviors.

Usually, when a family is expecting houseguests, they do some major cleaning. It can be a time to complete projects, dust in all the corners, prepare bedrooms for guests, or cook ahead of time and freeze the food. In addition, those closest to the deceased are likely to be grieving and need the presence of loved ones for support. I began asking for help, and one of the teenagers asked, "What do you want me to do — *stop living?* To his surprise, I answered, *"Yes!"*

Two of our adopted daughters live nearby, and I called to ask them to come over and help. One said, "But I hardly knew her! It's not a big deal to me!" My response was that it was a big deal to *me*, and I needed the loving support of my daughters in my time of grief. The other understood, *after* I explained it, and both eventually came and helped me catch up with housework and give their mom a few hugs.

Another difficulty surrounding this event was that it occurred in late May, at the height of graduation open houses, ceremonies, final exams, and so on. The three high school children had a hard time canceling *any* of their events, but we were able to reach some compromises. We discussed such things as who they should tell and how not to affect the party atmosphere by making the news public. In addition, missing a day of school the last week could seriously affect finals, grades, and so on, which meant I had to make some adjustments too and schedule the memorial service with those factors in mind.

Often such things don't come to mind until you're right in the midst of the moment. I found that I quickly became angry or resentful, largely due to my own close-to-the-surface emotions, when the teens questioned or objected. But in their defense, I hadn't taught them these things beforehand, so it was a new experience for them.

A death is not the only major event that fits this category. A wedding, a birth, a specific type of party — such as a "coming out" celebration, like a bar mitzvah or *quinceañera* — would all have certain expected social behaviors.

In some communities, you wouldn't attend a graduation open house without a gift. In others, it's assumed that all the teens making the rounds would bring a gift only to their close friends. Attire may be another issue at any social event, but at the more emotion-laden ones, it may become a bigger issue.

Discussing these things ahead of time — even attending a funeral or wake when it isn't an immediate family member — would be of great help to both you and your children. It could eliminate some of the emotional struggles between you and your children later when you need to be focusing on and *living* an event itself.

Having said all that, it's also true that sometimes **experience** is not only the best teacher, it's the *only* teacher. So don't beat yourself up if your youngsters and teenagers don't really understand the death and grieving process until they've been through it.

Another factor in working with older children — whether as a foster parent or an adoptive parent — is assessment. You'll probably be putting the teenager in therapy with a counselor or mental health worker. It will be your job to assist the therapist in determining what areas are deficient and where to put the emphasis in treatment. In addition, you'll be working on the same kinds of things at home, along with some more practical skills associated with independence.

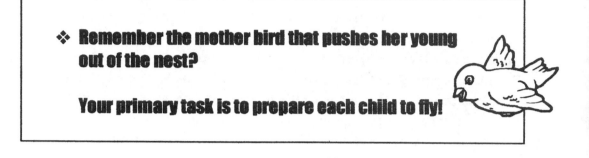

❖ **Remember the mother bird that pushes her young out of the nest?**

Your primary task is to prepare each child to fly!

We mature in many different ways, but there are five basic areas that you likely will be assessing and addressing. These are the **physical**, the **cognitive**, the **emotional**, the **social**, and the **moral** areas of development. These five come from the FosterPRIDE/AdoptPRIDE training program used in such states as Illinois and Michigan:

- **Physical** development includes size and ability. There are "strength" factors and "coordination" factors. These also would include fine-motor control, sense of balance, hand-eye coordination, and so on.
- The **cognitive** area is the ability to understand things, read, write, do math, and handle schoolwork.
- The **emotional** area has to do with feelings — and the ability to recognize and deal with them.
- The **social** area is about understanding relationships and how we interact with other people.
- The **moral** area of development is about conscience, knowledge of right and wrong, and acting appropriately within our society's (and family's) belief system.

As one who tries to live according to the teachings of Christ, I find it interesting that Luke 2:52 in the New Testament of the Bible says that "Jesus grew in wisdom and stature, and in favor with God and men." Four of the preceding five are covered!

A child can be ahead in one area, behind in another, and right on schedule in a third. Development often slows or even stops if a child receives a severe trauma — for example, loss of a parent, rape, witnessing violence, or some other crisis situation. This means that part of the child is left behind (sometimes termed arrested development), while the rest grows. An example would be a child who does fine academically, appears to be the age he/she is, makes friends among his/her peers, learns easily, but who has never developed a sense of right and wrong — a conscience. Moral development typically occurs between the ages of 4 and 7. Thus a child whose sexual abuse occurred at that age or stage, or whose parents died then, may be suffering from post-traumatic stress disorder and may be experiencing arrested development in the area of morality.

Another way children can be deficient in developing is when they are never taught certain ways of behaving or interacting with peers. Perhaps they don't know how to make friends. Perhaps they haven't been taught to figure things out logically and thus are poor problem solvers and decision makers. It may be that they didn't develop physically and have poor fine-motor coordination, clumsiness, or other physical limitations. One of the girls I adopted had great difficulty stepping from boulder to boulder alongside a lake, while the other (even younger) children in the family did it with ease.

In Appendix C of this book you'll find a sample assessment tool I developed. It's for parents to use when they're trying to determine if their child needs help in the decision-making area. The process includes observation, recording, analyzing data, and setting up a program to aid the child and reassessing how it works. Read it carefully and think of ways to assess another skill that your child seems to be having a problem with, then try it. There's a list of independent living skills with the assessment tool — to give you some ideas to start with. You should take careful note of this list and decide whether your child needs assistance in some areas.

If you prefer, you can buy an assessment tool or an entire independent living program, instead of custom-designing your own. The most common problem will be one of motivation. In my state all teens in the foster care system who are older than 15 must be in an independent living program or have a plan. It was easy to include my own children and teach them at the same time as the foster children. You should be thinking all the time about teaching your children adult skills. Make every experience at your home a *learning experience.* Soon your children will be armed with enough skills and knowledge to decide how they will live, what choices they have in a job market, and what types of friends they might choose.

Anger

Many foster and adopted children (especially older ones) are angry. Some show it in active ways, some in passive ones. Regarding a child who smashes a window with his fist, the anger is rather obvious. But one who deliberately fails classes (despite a high IQ), has a short temper, breaks house rules, and sabotages countless attempts to help him may be acting out his anger in a passive-aggressive way.

Why are these young people angry? There are so many reasons that I hardly know where to begin. Here are eight:

1. Loss of control over their life.
2. Forcibly moved away from friends and family.
3. Feelings of rejection by biological parents.
4. Feelings that bio-parents could have prevented the separation.
5. Belief that they don't deserve your loving-kindness and sacrifices on their behalf because they aren't "good enough" (feelings of worthlessness).
6. Learned behavior regarding the expression of one's anger. Children learn to behave by watching the way their parents behave. If Mom throws dishes when she's angry, they may do the same thing. If Dad punches a wall, they might also. We model our responses for our children, who watch every move we make!
7. Fear of being teased or rejected by classmates — or actually getting teased or rejected. So a "chip on the shoulder" becomes a defense. Many of my foster children entered

their new school with an "attitude." This was supposed to protect them against teasing or rejection by the kids in the new school.

8. Sheer frustration at the "hand" they've been dealt in life. This can take many forms, including:

    *   Feeling forced to change just about everything in their life against their will.
    *   Needing to give up the "old script" of life and having to learn a new one (no longer having their former role in their family, perhaps as the "parentified child" in charge or the caretaker).
    *   Perhaps giving up their role as "clown," whose job it was to distract others from the real problems.
    *   Maybe they were the baby of the family, cared for by everyone else.

What can you do to help these young people?

*   First, acknowledge their feelings. Validate them (the kids *and* their feelings). Make them feel heard and understood.
*   Second, accept the child anyway. Let him/her know that while you may not approve of the actions you understand the feelings and still love him/her.
*   Third, show the child acceptable ways to deal with anger and constructive ways to move through it and grow beyond it.

It will depend on the child and on you just how you do these things. You each have an individual style, and it's your job as the parent to reach the child with understanding and compassion.

I have generally chosen a time when no one is angry, and there's no pressure on either the child or me. Then I open a discussion by being up front about what I'm trying to do. After restating Steps 1 and 2 above, I tell the child or teen it's unacceptable to demonstrate anger by smashing a window with his fist (or whatever he has been doing). I explain that he may have totally legitimate reasons for anger but that he must learn more appropriate ways of dealing with it. Then I make some suggestions and provide some role models — or even have him "play act" with me.

Sometimes it's helpful to analyze what the child has done in the past and try to come up with a new way of expressing himself that uses some part of that behavior and *the same body part* the young person used. For example:

- A child or teen who kicks things in anger should be encouraged to use his feet in an activity like running, sports where he kicks a ball, calisthenics that use feet, and so on.
- A child or teen who hits things can be given harmless things to hit: a punching bag, a pillow, a baseball, or a volleyball — or an even more violent activity like a sledgehammer to use on a junk car. In addition, this child should be told, in no uncertain terms, what assault is and what the punishment for it is in the adult world.
- A child or teen who defaces property should be taught to refinish wood furniture, build things, or otherwise construct, rather than destruct.
- A child or teen who uses verbal anger — such as profanity, threats, yelling, and so on — should be taught to say or write about what is angering him. This will provide an outlet and help him put a feeling into concrete terms to be dealt with. Caution this child about oral or written threats and their consequences in this day of terrorism, laws against any type of aggressive behavior in schools, or even suspicion of threats or aggression.

Many schools or communities have anger management classes. If they don't, seek help from the child's therapist, school counselor, or any mentor the child has. Exaggerate your role modeling in the area of anger management and be sure your child *knows he/she has a choice.* I can't count the number of times I have heard, "It wasn't *my* fault. He *made* me mad! He knows I have a short temper. He shouldn't have made me so mad."

Children will never get control over anger if they don't believe *they have control over these behaviors* to begin with. Often these kids have major control issues, and that's exactly where I deal with it. I explain that they are admitting that another person has control over their innermost feelings — even over their future. I encourage them to regain control by using appropriate means of expressing anger. I stress *choice and responsibility. Never* allow a child to place blame on anyone else for his actions. Let him know you expect him to make choices based on thought, maturity, and his new skills in anger management. Most of them can live up to your expectations!

Role models are very important in anger management. We all watched our parents when they were angry and *learned* ways of expressing that anger — for better or for worse. So get your *own* house in order before trying to teach others!

When *you* are angry, don't suppress it but instead model ways of expressing it appropriately. After all, if you punch a guy in the nose at work because he insulted you, it is *you* who will lose your job (and maybe even be taken to court), not the other guy! And you can enlist teachers to help with follow-through at school. Ask for a meeting, set up a behavior contract, and think of appropriate rewards for good anger management and restraint.

Another great way to control anger is to sign your child up for **karate** (or tae kwon do). Karate is a common remedy for children with ADHD to gain self-control, and it has worked wonders for my son who has bipolar disorder and oppositional defiant disorder. In the past he slammed doors, threw things, hit the wall, argued, broke things, and totally lost control of himself in fights with the family. However, since he has started karate classes, he has not only learned *physical* ways to deal with anger, he has learned a philosophy of self-control, constructive thought, meditation, and *responsibility for his own actions.*

In addition, he has made some very close friends who function as his "family" and a personal support system. They are forthright and can be judgmental, but they share deep love and respect for each other and a new respect for the wisdom that age and experience bring to the adults in their life. Learning a martial art has taught thousands of children with attention deficit disorder to *focus.* It has provided a means of introspection and self-understanding. It lends itself to rigorous activity — but with a goal and purpose. It pits competitive kids against themselves. It gives individuals a skill they can be proud of among their peers. It teaches a youth how to fight but also *not* to fight, except in clear cases of self-defense.

Yet another excellent activity for boys and girls who need to channel their aggression — and learn to focus — is **chess**. Numerous studies show that this ancient game of skill and strategy teaches kids how to think, to concentrate, to solve problems. Yet, like karate, chess is played in competitive arena where sportsmanship and etiquette are emphasized.

Ask your children's therapist for additional suggestions. He/she may have ideas you can try with your children, as well as behavior management suggestions for both them and you.

Finally, if you foster or adopt older teens, be sure to take a look at Appendix A. It lists reasons why it might be wise for them to stay under parental "protection" somewhat longer than a biological child might. It isn't until age 25 that the average American young person becomes truly independent, yet most of us are in the habit of sending our foster children out into the world when they may have even fewer life skills than the average youth of the same age. Additional guidelines to help determine readiness for independent living are found in Appendix B.

CHAPTER 23

Dealing with 'Failure'

Whose failure do you need to deal with — yours or your child's? Both!

New parents — whether biological, foster, adoptive, or surrogate — tend to blame themselves for any failure of their child. In addition, they may feel *they* are failures in the eyes of such service providers as teachers, doctors, social workers, or judges. Workers and licensers should take note of this section! Newly licensed foster parents often attempt to "succeed" by themselves, without adequate knowledge and experience, instead of seeking help. Then if their foster care placement becomes unbearable or unworkable, they finally give up and ask to have the child removed from their home.

Programmed for failure

Some children have spent their entire life believing they're "worthless," "destined for failure," and "stupid." These labels are deeply embedded in their self-image. If they somehow manage to succeed at something, or do something "smart" instead of stupid, it sets up a conflict in their brain called "cognitive dissonance." In other words, the event or image doesn't "fit." One of my first fostering experiences was with such a boy, and *his* problem eventually became *mine!*

"Will" was only a month from graduation, and he would be the very first teenager in the history of his family to graduate from high school. I had no idea this event could have such a tremendous impact on him because *everyone* in *my* family graduated. It was a completely normal event — in fact not even a momentous one — on the way to college.

But inside Will was a perfect example of "cognitive dissonance," with a virtual tornado of emotion whirling around. To complicate matters even further, he and his girlfriend of three years had just broken up, and he was devastated. Then, three weeks before commencement exercises, he borrowed a friend's car, picked up a buddy and two girls they hardly knew, and began to drive.

These four teens bought alcohol, filled the gas tank, turned the radio up, and headed out of town to "who knows where?" They ended up several hundred miles away, broke into a cabin that one of the girls knew of, and began a weeklong party that ended in disaster.

Throughout the week the boys broke into 13 more cabins in the area, stole alcohol, food, stereo equipment and tapes, and anything else they thought looked like fun. By then, of course, an APB (all points bulletin) had been issued by police, and a multi-state search for them was in progress. There also were several sets of very worried parents (not to mention an angry car owner).

Eventually Will simply walked in the front door, announcing to us that he was home and headed for bed. Uh-uh. Not so fast!

We had to call the police, report that he was back, deal with the car and the other kids, and try to find out what had happened. It turned into a very long night. In the end, Will went to jail, not commencement, and followed in his family's footsteps. While he later got a GED (General Educational Development) diploma, the prospect of impending success conflicted so much with his self-image (of failure) that he just couldn't handle it.

But the story didn't end there. After Will left, my husband and I experienced such a tremendous feeling of loss and failure we had no idea how to deal with it. And the foster care caseworker typically "follows the child," meaning we heard nothing more from her for weeks.

At last, I called the agency and asked her to come out and talk. As new foster parents, we felt we had let the agency down, let Will's parents down, let Will down, and were unfit to take another child. We figured it was time to throw in the towel, so we wanted her to come and get our license.

That worker spent the afternoon with us soon after my call. We talked and talked. She supported, reinforced, explained, and generally lifted us back up, convincing us that we had no reason to quit and were actually doing a fine job. She pointed out that Will, a young adult, had made some choices over which we had no control.

I never forgot that lesson when I became a foster care caseworker. It's part of the reason I advocate so strongly for a support system, a network, and a shoulder to lean on (and, in some cases, cry on) for new foster parents.

And after a child left (no matter for what reason), I never failed to call his/her foster home, just to check on how those parents were doing.

All new parents need mentors and support

When I was a caseworker, I received a call early one Monday morning from a newly licensed foster parent who had taken a teenage girl the previous week. The woman was in tears after having cut her ankle-length hair to shoulder-length because she had gotten lice from her foster child! It was very unfortunate that she had never had any experience with lice before — *and* that she had no one she was comfortable to call on a weekend. While the situation seemed both funny and sad to *me*, it was clearly traumatic to *her*. I explained some remedies for lice to her, all the while wondering about the wisdom of telling prospective parents the liabilities that might come with their children. Would this discourage them from getting lice-ensed?!

The other thing I did for her was to let her know that in the future she could call on anyone in the foster parent support group at any time of day or night if she had a problem that was that traumatic. And I followed up the discussion with a home visit a few days later to see if my advice had worked for the family. We've been friends ever since. And, at this writing, her hair has grown most of the way back!

Parents of special needs children learn to be thankful for the small victories. They measure time in shorter intervals. They take joy in a word or action that indicates a child is trying hard to learn.

❖ **Remember: medication, therapy, and behavior modification.**

In short, a multi-faceted approach "works like a gem."

For example, suppose you designed a behavior contract with your teenager around his use of profanity. In the beginning you might ask him to refrain from using profanity for a day at a time, rewarding him if he could do it. Later the reward would come for a week without swearing, and finally the rewards would be removed, and a new behavior would be addressed.

Or maybe you're working at nightly incontinence (bed-wetting), which is one sign of possible sexual abuse when not age-appropriate. If children are able to get up and go to the bathroom during the night, they should be rewarded. If they make it to morning without wetting or soiling, they should be rewarded. Or perhaps they never succeed in curing this behavior (and some of them don't), then focus on teaching them to wash their bedding, shower before school, and simply take care of the problem without offending others. For this child, and for you, this will be success.

What does "failure" mean to children?
- Perhaps they get failing grades.
- Perhaps they can't please you.
- Perhaps they're shunned by their peers at school.

I don't believe in "sheltering" children from criticism. I don't think the ego is such a fragile thing that I can never correct a child. What is more important is to teach him/her how to cope with failure and turn it around.

Here are some examples. You and your child will need to be creative and perhaps work as a team to solve some problems, but you can take care of many of them yourself. Here's how Dr. Ruby Payne handled one child.

1. **Do some problem solving with the child.** "Why are you failing?" (The answer may surprise you.) *"If I get good grades, my friends will get on my case."*

2. **Find out if the child is motivated to change.** Ask! *"Heck no, only geeks get A's."*

3. **Do some goal setting with the child.** "What can you do about it? Could you try for C's and B's? What if no one knew about your higher grades?"

4. **Assist the child with the solution.** Maintain good follow-through. Set up a plan for good grades and find a way to keep them confidential. In addition, if a child needs to learn study skills, you can teach those.

Let's tackle another one. Children shouldn't feel that they can never please you. You should be celebrating success at every opportunity. However, some children are perfectionists, and it's really themselves they're trying to please. This is an issue to tackle with the therapist. But you can reinforce the success story anytime they do anything for you. In addition, I've heard many parents criticize and yell at their children day in and day out, and such children learn to shield themselves and to always feel they have failed. A child like this may even believe they have caused their parent to abuse them — because "I was bad," or "Daddy wouldn't have to drink if I didn't drive him crazy." These children should be taught who is really responsible for the behavior and that they don't have any control over their parents.

The third example was that the child is being shunned by peers. Sit down and evaluate the problem with the child. Seek input from teachers or playground supervisors. Address the problems one by one.

1. Is the child interacting with other children in a manner they're used to? Does she dress in a radically different way?
2. Is the child defensive, or does she have a "chip on her shoulder"?
3. Is the child threatening to the others?
4. Does the child try to build herself up by telling untrue stories?
5. Is the child a "tattletale" or "narc"?
6. Is the child handicapped or have odd or disgusting behaviors?
7. Does the school overlook ridicule and criticism that occurs there?
8. Are the teachers and administrators appropriate role models?
9. Does the child perceive the reactions of others accurately?
10. Does the child lack social skills?

Once you have determined the reasons for the girl being shunned, you can address the issues with her by goal setting and behavior modification. In addition, you should work as a team with the teachers, with appropriate goal setting and reassessment. Children can be taught social skills.

If the child is resistant, because the behaviors aren't acceptable in the place she came from, help her learn to use a different set of behaviors in different settings. Explain the "hidden rules" to her — rules that will allow her to make friends in her new neighborhood, yet allow her to switch back to the old ways when visiting or returning to the original one. Present them as "tools" to give her power and control over peer acceptance, as well as knowledge she will use as an adult on a job.

Finally, don't forget that children may not see themselves as a failure, even if you do. If no one in their family has ever graduated from high school, they won't be considered a failure if they don't graduate. But for you, this may be a failure.

So you can see that "failure" is a relative term. After 19 years of fostering, I was never designated "Foster Parent of the Year" by either my agency or the State Foster Parent Association. For me, this was a failure because it had been a goal of mine. However, the number of foster children I helped, the number of foster parents I supported, and the number of crises I responded to should certainly qualify me as a successful foster/parent and foster care worker. In fact, it does — in the eyes of my own peers.

When my husband and I recently retired from fostering, I closed a chapter of my life. But there was no retirement party, no transition, and no recognition of "a job well-done." Earlier I acknowledged that I have a need for external recognition. My husband has no such need and is satisfied with what he does and how he does it, whether anyone recognizes it or not. How well do *you* cope? What about your child?

CHAPTER 24

Rewards

Most of the rewards of parenting other people's children are very personal. They include the rewards of raising children that all parents receive, whether biological or not. Parents pass on a part of themselves to and in their children and, as such, they touch immortality. Genetically and otherwise, they have had an impact on future generations — for better or worse. We hope, of course, "for better."

In addition, to assess the reward, parents must examine the original reasons they began to parent and see if they reached goals and satisfied their own needs.

Perhaps you took another child to satisfy your own nurturing needs and the instinct to parent. Or perhaps you decided life was empty without a child in the house. Or maybe you discovered you were infertile after marrying, and your dream of a family was unfulfilled.

Was your reason the need to help someone? Or perhaps you were asked to do it by someone else, such as the court, a relative, or a friend. Did you feel you *had* to take in a child because of something your own son or daughter was doing (drug or alcohol abuse?), and you already had formed a relationship with the grandchild?

Does your peer group or community believe it is the responsibility of all its members to care for the children in the community? Is it your strong religious belief and feeling that it's a ministry God has called you to? Do you believe it's your "destiny" or reason for being here?

All these reasons and more are given to licensers when people inquire about becoming foster parents. In the past, society simply absorbed parent-less children in many informal ways. But in today's society, the "system" demands proper paperwork and appropriate placements, as well as legal rights for all. Therefore, surrogate parenting continues, as it always has before, only now more formally.

The rewards can be numerous. A child may tug at your heartstrings and convince you of the need to take him/her in. Your self-image may be incomplete if you cannot parent, so raising a family is fulfilling. If it's a ministry, satisfaction is derived from knowing you are doing what God wants you to do.

Many parents stay in touch with their children throughout a lifetime, and some do not. When one of my many foster children returns to tell me how he/she is doing, it's a testimony to my efforts to keep them from failing. By caring for our granddaughter, my husband and I believe we may be able to stop a cycle of poverty, pregnancy, and failure that has existed for many generations in our adopted daughter's family. And by adopting her at the age of 18, we knew all we could do for her was provide a "safety net" for her adult life — and a place to call "home" during holidays and major events in her life.

The rewards of parenting are too many to mention and too personal to be relevant to everyone reading this book. It's my hope that the book will lend insight and strength to all parents in their efforts to have an impact on the lives of their children and the generation growing up in today's complex world. As caseworkers become more overloaded and systems more impersonal, we all need the advice of our friends.

In these pages I hope I have proved to be a friend to you. Blessings to you as you consider — or continue — the grand adventure of *Parenting Someone Else's Child.*

Appendix A

Blocks for teens to becoming independent

1. Fear (don't deny it).
2. Denial (don't deny denial either!). ☺
3. Lack of knowledge and training.
4. Drugs and alcohol.
5. Lack of ability or aptitude.
6. Low self-esteem or lack of confidence.
7. Unresolved feelings about biological family.
8. Few positive role models.
9. Lack of time to prepare.
10. Immaturity.
11. Depression due to lack of planning and follow-through.
12. Victim mentality.

Appendix B

Practical skills for independent living

This list is certainly not comprehensive. You will want to add to it as you think of more skills.

- Obtaining utilities.
- Traveling to work.
- Traveling by reading a map.
- Decision-making skills.
- Knowledge of foods and nutrition.
- Knowledge of childcare and discipline.
- Knowing what constitutes an emergency — and knowing who to call for help, when to call, and how to call.
- Understanding a lease.
- Understanding the legal implications of signing a contract.
- Obtaining insurance — auto, renters, and health insurance.
- Changing a flat tire!
- Knowing when a "good deal" is really a scam.

- Establishing your own support system of friends, church family, biological family, and others who can enjoy your company and help when you need it.
- Understanding money management and credit, which includes paying bills, making a budget, saving for emergencies, and requesting assistance from providers (if unemployed).
- Judging when to go to a doctor, when to go to the emergency room, when to ask a pharmacist.
- Finding a doctor, dentist, or other professional — and getting there.
- Finding service providers, such as plumbers, electricians, garbage haulers, construction workers.
- Others?

Appendix C

Sample assessment

Decision-making skills

I. Assess

1. Foster parent notices child goes to several stores for one item but can't make up mind.

2. Child agonizes for an hour about whether to go with friends to movie or go with family to graduation party.

3. Child takes turn planning dinner; cannot figure out what to make.

4. Foster parent designs simple quiz. Child takes very long time to make decisions on relatively easy items.

5. Foster parent deliberately sets up situations and notes that child cannot make general decisions on normal family issues as well or quickly as rest of family.

6. Foster parent has household fire drill and notices that child panics in indecision over which exit to take.

7. Child is making poor choices at school and in picking friends.

8. Foster parent brings observations to therapist, who says he/she has noticed same pattern.

9. Foster parent talks to teachers about child's decision-making abilities; they confirm foster parent's perceptions.

10. Foster parent questions bio-parent. Same story at home. Difficulty making decisions.

II. Motivate

1. Foster parent shows or tells child results of assessment and asks child for input/opinion. Child becomes defensive. Foster parent calms child and reassures him/her that no marks, criticism, or other negative is intended but that this difficulty can be corrected, if child wants to.

2. Foster parent and child look at possible reasons for difficulty, as well as problems that could arise from difficulty in making decisions.

3. Foster parent and child look at possible benefits from correcting problem.

4. Foster parent and child begin designing plan; suggestion is made to seek additional input.

5. Possible rewards are discussed.

III. Plan

1. Gather team members and child; decide upon and begin designing plan.
    a. List goals. *Final goal is always "Child knows where to go for assistance, if he/she runs into difficulty."*
    b. List steps to goals (end results expected).
    c. List assessment method.
    d. Clarify rewards for child, adding temporary external ones if needed.

2. Write down plans. Everyone signs and keeps copy for reference. If this is foster child, be sure caseworker has copy of plan. If this is legal guardianship, it's good to put this item into court file. The plan may be included in quarterly report.

IV. Document

1. As child works through learning process, be sure to reassess and document progress. Visuals help child see his/her own progress. (See examples in Appendix E.)

2. Be sure to build up child, giving rewards and motivation as needed.

3. When goals are reached, program is ended. *When out on his/her own, it is essential for child to know where to go for help.*

V. Recognize progress

1. Do final documentation for caseworker and praise child for jobs well-done! See Chapter 24 for more on rewards.

2. A certificate of completion for child's portfolio or life book would be appropriate, as well as special dinner, cake, or celebration. Design certificate. Again, see Chapter 24.

Appendix D

In case of emergency

The children in your home need to know how to handle emergencies, no matter what their age. There should be a sheet near the phone with the following information on it. *All* foster homes should have one, as the children coming in and out won't be expected to know this information!

9-1-1

Family name: Mr. and Mrs. Foster Parent
Address: 4 Agency Avenue
Cross streets: Avenue A & Avenue B SW
Our phone number: (999) 555-0000
Dad's work number: 555-1111
Doctor: Dr. Careforyou: 555-2222
Who lives here: John F. Parent and Mary F. Parent
        Joe Oldest, 18
        Sister Sue, 16
        John Foster, 14
        Harry Foster, 13
Foster care worker: Mary Worker: 555-3333
Nearest neighbor: Harry Helpful: 555-4444

Appendix E

Helping the child see his/her own progress

	Sunday	Monday	Tuesday	Wednesday	Thursday	Friday	Saturday
Up on time	☆	☆	☆		☆	☆	☆
Fed dog	☆	☆		☆			☆
Clean Rm.		☆	☆		☆	☆	☆

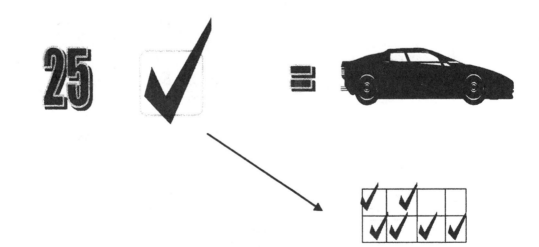

(Move turtle along as child nears goal.)

Use your imagination to come up with more ideas. Give pennies, tokens, coupons, or other tangible rewards, especially to young children.

Appendix F

Confidentiality and mandated reporting

When you become a licensed foster parent, two important legal matters must be considered:

- Confidentiality.
- Mandated reporting of suspected abuse.

All children who come into the home of a licensed foster parent have a personal history. They are placed under court jurisdiction either because they have been delinquent or because of neglect or abuse. These children and their families have the right to privacy, and you will be obligated to respect that right. You are under the same confidentiality restrictions as their foster care and delinquency workers, and any other licensed professionals who deal with them. At times, this can be a difficult restriction.

The only people who have a right to know your child's case history and personal details are those directly involved with his/her care or legally involved with the family. These may be the child's therapist, doctor, teacher, probation officer, or caseworker. And others may have the right to *limited* information but not all information.

You will find that some friends, family, and neighbors are curious. They will ask you why the child has been placed in your home and what his/her background is. Teachers will ask personal questions — and your own children will want to know things. *But you are obligated to keep details confidential as much as possible, and so are your children!* With instructions from you, the biological children in a foster home soon learn to fend off the curiosity of their classmates and friends.

Some details may be necessary to share with school officials, but these must be limited to only what is necessary for the child's health and safety. You can say, "Joey got into some trouble where he used to live, and we want to give him a chance to start over." Another idea with school officials might be: "Joey has a problem with anger control, so teachers should be alert to finding ways to help him with this." My own children were sometimes unaware that we took in kids who had committed violent crimes — *if* I felt that the crimes had no bearing on our household.

At times we also took children (for short-term placements) who lived in our own neighborhood. Some had well-known parents in our town. On occasion we had to say a child "was just visiting us for a while" in order to protect a delicate situation. But other times more details were shared regarding such factors as learning disabilities or dangerous behaviors (like fire-setting, sexual aggression, or making false reports of abuse). If you're ever in doubt as to what you should share in various settings, ask your caseworker or a more experienced foster parent.

People — including school officials and staff — are naturally curious. After a while, I learned whom to contact when registering a new student. And if someone asked an inappropriate question, I would simply say I couldn't answer it.

In this book we discussed the team approach to care, and certain team members will have copies of reports and details that others may not need. For example, a medical doctor will want any psychological reports and physical data, as well as behavior reports and anything that will involve medication or other care-related details. But a mentor for the child will not need those details. One or two teachers may need copies of school evaluations, behavior records, and a possible special needs diagnosis, but all the teachers in the school do not need these things. A school counselor or principal may need certain sensitive details, but these facts and factors don't need to be shared with the entire staff.

Confidentiality is very important; you could even lose your license for not respecting it. Gossiping about case histories, telling abuse details over coffee, or shrugging when your children reveal these things ... all are highly inappropriate. As in the case of not allowing a sexual abuse victim or perpetrator to baby sit for the neighbors, you may tell only what is absolutely necessary, and in almost all cases that is *nothing!* You may simply tell the neighbor who's looking for a sitter that you *don't allow it.* Period. If you need to warn male teachers not to be in a room alone with a female student, say as little as possible – just give the warning. It's hard, but it's necessary. And it *is* a matter of *law.*

Another matter of law is that of "mandated reporting." This phrase means that certain licensed professionals, such as doctors, teachers, therapists, and *you,* the licensed foster parent, are *required* to report any known *or suspected* abuse to the authorities. An example might be a foster child who returns from a home visit with unexplained bruises. Another could be a teen who confides in you that she felt uncomfortable with how her uncle touched her recently. Yes, even *suspected* abuse must be reported. You should receive pre-service training in your foster parent classes that will teach you what signs of abuse you should watch for. Be observant and ask questions about anything you're unsure of.

More detailed information should be given to you in your training classes. If it isn't made available, be sure to ask for it.

Appendix G

A glossary of terms, jargon, and 'alphabet soup' — all made clear!

ADD (attention deficit disorder): A term used to describe certain characteristics in a person who has difficulty concentrating, remembering, and following through, among other things.

ADHD (attention deficit hyperactivity disorder): Same as ADD, but an individual with ADHD is also hyperactive. Many people use these two terms interchangeably, but they are quite different.

Agencies and agency types: Agencies associated with foster and adoptive care include many social services agencies (each state has a different name, such as Family Independence Agency, Welfare Office, etc.). Examples include:

- *Private agencies,* such as Bethany Christian Services, Catholic Social Services, etc., which supervise adoptions or do foster care.
- *Residential facilities,* which house foster children considered too dangerous or mentally ill to reside in the community.
- *Adoption referral agencies,* which only make referrals and don't process adoptions.
- Private or publicly run *shelter homes,* which take children initially placed in foster care and assess them for more permanent homes.
- *Group foster homes,* defined by the state they're in, but they're usually limited to 6-8 youths and have more formal rules and supervision standards than a regular home.
- *Secured detention,* like a jail for juveniles.
- *Unsecured detention,* a home or institution where young people are placed; it's like jail except not locked, has 24-hour

supervisory staff, and has school within the premises (similar to a "minimum security prison").

Attorney: May be prosecuting attorney (often abbreviated atty), who brings the case against a delinquent, or defense atty (court-appointed or not) who represents the youth in court hearings.

Bipolar disorder: One of only three personality disorders that are chemically based. Formerly called manic-depressive, these individuals experience wide mood swings and activity levels, as well as episodes of euphoria and depression they can't control without medication.

Board and care rates vs. personal allowance rates: Foster parents receive several kinds of payment reimbursements. The monthly checks represent both money to house/feed a child and money for the child's personal needs. Agencies typically determine whether children receive their personal need money or the foster parent keeps it to take care of their needs for them. Your agency will define and break down your payments for you if you ask.

CASA (court-appointed special advocate): Child's advocate from the community who has received specialized training for volunteers, is appointed by the court, and who follows an individual abuse or neglect case. The advocate makes recommendations to the foster care workers and the court and also makes a specified number of contacts with the child throughout the duration of the case.

Case manager or foster care worker: The worker assigned to a foster care, adoption, or delinquency case who is directly responsible for case management. This usually entails creating a case plan and making all contacts with anyone associated with the child, as well as writing reports to the court or contracting agency.

CD (conduct disorder): Mental health term used to describe a child whose conduct is markedly deviant from the norm and whose behavior warrants professional intervention because the individual has come into the realm of lawbreaking in the community. (Before breaking any laws, the individual often is said to have oppositional defiant disorder.)

Contracted case: A protective services, delinquency, or regular foster care case that is handled by someone other than the original receiving agency. For example, a private foster care agency might manage the case of a delinquent placed in foster care *for* the court, which pays the agency to do the work, make placement decisions, and write reports.

Court hearings: Delinquent foster children and abusive parents attend a series of court hearings throughout the duration of their case. Some examples are *preliminary hearing, adjudication, dispositional hearing, review hearing, permanency planning hearing, termination hearing.* Foster parents should understand the definition and purpose of these hearings, as well as their role in any hearing involving their child. Contact the court or agency you are working with for detailed information.

CPS (Child Protective Services): Office within the social services agency responsible for taking and evaluating complaints of child abuse or neglect — and deciding whether to pursue the complaint. Officials in this office investigate allegations and recommend solutions to problems that have come to their attention.

Criminal records check vs. background check: When an individual applies for a license to do foster care, two kinds of investigations are done. One checks general background data, while the other checks for actual crimes they may have committed, including criminal sexual conduct.

CSC (criminal sexual conduct): The crime of sexually assaulting or abusing someone to varying degrees, labeled CSC-1 through CSC-4. This includes not only rape, but all forms of sexual contact and activity, such as pornographic photography, exposing children to pornography, etc.

DO/MD/DDS (Doctor of Osteopathy, Medical Doctor, Doctor of Dental Surgery): Designations or titles for different types of doctors. Each has received a different type of training.

DOC (difficulty of care) levels and rates: Some states have rating systems to determine the level of care needed for a child and the rate the foster/adoptive parent will be paid for that care. A thorough understanding of the rating system is necessary for an understanding of a child's behaviors, physical and emotional needs, and the subsidies you will receive and why.

DSM (Diagnostic and Statistical Manual of Mental Disorders): For mental health professionals, published by the American Psychiatric Association. (Each update gets a new number, such as DSM-III, DSM-IV, etc.) Contains exact definitions and diagnostic criteria for mental health disorders. Also used by doctors and insurance companies, special education personnel, and many others.

Encopresis/encopretic: Lack of control over bowels (bowel movements in pants or bed). *Sometimes* a sign of sex abuse.

Enuresis/enuretic: Lack of control over bladder (bed-wetting).

FAS (fetal alcohol syndrome): Physical outcome in babies caused by maternal *or* paternal alcohol consumption just prior to, or during, pregnancy. Symptoms are defined in the DSM-IV. There's also fetal alcohol effect (FAE), with lesser but still significant characteristics.

Forms: As foster care and adoption is regulated by the government, the foster or adoptive parent will become familiar with many kinds of forms. It's important to use them correctly and to *maintain a case file for each child.* Talk to your licensing worker about this.

Foster care vs. delinquency vs. voluntary types of placements: The state defines cases differently and dictates different procedures for them. For additional detail, see Appendix H.

- "Regular" foster care is for children who have been abused, neglected, or abandoned.
- "Delinquent" foster care is for youths who have been judged guilty of breaking the law and are under adult supervision as a consequence of it.
- "Voluntary" placements may include parental requests, crisis intervention placements, certain short-term cases, or others in which parents pay the bill. These placements are usually very short.
- "Medically fragile" placements are those where a child requires a great deal of care for medical needs, and the parents generally receive substantial reimbursement.
- "Mental health" placements may be funded by a mental health agency and are usually for the parents' respite (or rest) from caring for a high-needs child. Such placements help keep a child in the parental home instead of an institution.

HIV (human immunodeficiency virus) vs. AIDS (acquired immunodeficiency syndrome): HIV is the virus that causes AIDS, while AIDS is the disease itself. It is characterized by lack of immunity to disease and can be caused by transfer of blood or bodily fluids from one person to another, usually through sexual contacts or needle sharing by drug addicts (or accidental needle pricks in healthcare settings).

ISP (initial service plan): Document that is required within 30 days of a child's placement in foster care or delinquency care; it includes an assessment and recommendations for the treatment plan and goals (see USP).

LTP (live-together partner): Term used by social workers to describe a person's "significant other," "common law spouse," homosexual partner, roommate, et al.

Medicare vs. Medicaid and Primary Care Physicians (PCPs) vs. open Medicaid: We won't go into specifics here, but you need to know that foster children have a different kind of Medicaid than others. It's called "open" because they don't have a designated primary care provider since most of them move so often.

Mental health therapist: Individual who does counseling in a mental health setting, such as a hospital, community mental health agency, or private practice.

- There are many different degrees and sets of qualifications for therapists; the consumer should investigate licensure and qualifications for anyone he/she receives counseling from. Examples are: psychiatrists; psychologists; licensed social workers of varying levels; limited license psychologists; marriage counselors; priests, ministers, and other religious personnel trained in psychotherapy; school counselors and social workers; crisis intervention workers; and many more.
- In addition, there are individuals who provide limited counseling or advising, such as parent/therapists, crisis workers, religious priests and pastors who are *not* in a certified specialty, counselors at rape and women's centers, and others.
- Some therapists specialize in such areas as attachment disorders, marriage counseling, abuse, adoption, etc.

ODD (oppositional defiant disorder): Childhood disorder characterized by general defiant and disobedient behaviors more severe than the norm, usually coupled with a great deal of anger. The DSM contains an exact definition. This disorder is said to precede conduct disorder in most children.

PO (probation officer): Assigned by the court to oversee an individual who has committed a crime.

Reimbursements vs. pay and tax issues: Most foster parents are paid *after* child has stayed with them; thus they're being reimbursed for their care. Most adoptive homes are paid *before* the month the child stays in their home, thus giving them money to provide for their child. Sometimes foster parents also can be reimbursed for mileage, clothing, or special items needed by the child. Always check your tax laws to discover whether you must count the money as income. Usually, it is *not.* But if the funds are to be counted as income, then deductions from them are legal, the same as for biological children. If you feel you have legitimate tax deductions, consult a tax expert *who is familiar with foster care issues.*

USP (updated service plan): Quarterly report on child placed in foster care or delinquency care (see ISP).

Special education designations

Foster parents should become familiar with these terms:

AI: autism impairment
CI: cognitively impaired
ECDD: early childhood developmental delay
EI: emotionally impaired
EMI: educably mentally impaired
HI: hearing impaired
IEP: individual educational planning
IEPC: individual educational planning conference
LD: learning disability
MI: mentally impaired
MiMH: mildly mentally handicapped
MoMH: moderately mentally handicapped
PI: physically impaired
SLI: speech and language impaired
SXI: severely multiply impaired
TBI: traumatic brain injury
VI: visually impaired

Appendix H

Types of foster care

Medically fragile children: Those who need constant medical care.

Pregnant and parenting teens: Some teens are placed in foster care before or after the birth of their baby or babies.

Pre-adoptive placements: Children who are slated for adoption by a family but who (child and family) are still in the assessment or "trial" period.

Delinquent youths: Those placed in care by a court; these youths either have been convicted of a crime or crimes — or have been charged.

Neglected or abused children: Those under the jurisdiction of Child Protective Services and placed due to abuse, neglect, or both.

Therapy homes: Settings where the foster parents are especially trained to assist with therapy for disturbed foster children. Parents are required to document and collaborate, follow a detailed case or behavior plan, and provide intensive supervision and behavior evaluation or modification.

Group homes: Settings licensed for five or six foster children (may include up to eight children *under 18,* including the parents' own children and the foster children).

Emotionally impaired children: Those who, due to emotional impairment, require more intensive care but who have no specific medical needs.

Physically impaired children: Those with physical impairments, *not designated as medically fragile,* such as blindness, deafness, and paralysis, any of which would require special care.

Independent living placements: Older youths, usually ages 17 to 19, who need assistance in gaining independent living skills in a licensed or unlicensed foster home, which serves as a "halfway house" setting.

Shelter care placements: Children who are placed for *short-term* periods until an appropriate match or placement can found. This can be an institution or private home. Foster parents may or may not be paid to hold a bed open. These placements might be risky, as little or nothing may be known about the child — and they may come with lice, disease, emotional problems, just the clothes on their back, etc. Occasionally certain children repeatedly enter shelter care as they break more permanent placements, or they are repeatedly removed from their own home by Child Protective Services. These children often are quite difficult to care for.

There are, to be sure, even more types of foster care, if one includes secured and unsecured detention, residential care, adult foster care, and mental health hospitalization. So if you're new to foster care, don't be bashful about asking questions!

Bibliography *

* It would be impossible to list all the literature and people who have influenced and educated me. This bibliography constitutes the most significant and current sourcing as this book was being prepared in the summer of 2003.

–Ann Stressman

By author

Amen, Daniel G. (1995). *Windows into the ADD Mind: Understanding and Treating Attention Deficit Disorders in the Everyday Lives of Children, Teenagers and Adults.* Fairfield, CA: Mind Works Press.

Anderson, Robert (1997). *Section 504 Meetings: How Can They Help Your Child? (cassette tape).* Associated Interventions & Counseling. Ogden, UT. (800) 393-7138.

Armstrong, Thomas. (1995). *The Myth of the ADD Child: 50 Ways to Improve Your Child's Behavior and Attention Span Without Drugs, Labels, or Coercion.* New York, NY: Dutton.

Barkley, Russell A., & Benton, Christine M. (1998). *Your Defiant Child: Eight Steps to Better Behavior.* New York, NY: Guilford Press.

Benson, Peter L., Espeland, Pamela, & Galbraith, Judy. (1995). *What Kids Need to Succeed.* Minneapolis, MN: Free Spirit Publishing.

Cline, Foster W., & Fay, Jim. (1990). *Parenting With Love and Logic: Teaching Children Responsibility.* Colorado Springs, CO: Piñon Press.

Dobson, James. (1978). *The Strong-Willed Child: Birth Through Adolescence.* Wheaton, IL: Tyndale House.

Everett, Craig A. (1999). *Family Therapy for ADHD: Treating Children, Adolescents, and Adults.* New York, NY: Guilford Press.

Foster PRIDE/Adopt PRIDE. Program for teaching foster and adoptive parents. (1993). Illinois Department of Children & Family Services and Child Welfare League of America, in collaboration with and with assistance from several other agencies.

Hallowell, Edward M., & Ratey, John J. (1994). *Driven to Distraction.* New York, NY: Pantheon Books.

Hartmann, Thom. (1997). *Attention Deficit Disorder: A Different Perception.* Grass Valley, CA: Underwood Books.

Kubler-Ross, Elisabeth. (1997). *On Death and Dying.* New York, NY: Scribner Classics.

McCarney, Stephen B., & Bauer, Angela M. (1995). *The Parents' Guide to Attention Deficit Disorders.* Columbia, MO: Hawthorne Educational Services.

Mulder, E.J.H., Robles de Medina, P.G., Huizink, A.C., Van den Bergh, B.R.H., Buitelaar, J.K., & Visser, G.H.A. (2002). Prenatal maternal stress: effects on pregnancy and the (unborn) child. *Early Human Development,* 70, 3-14.

Payne, Ruby K. (2003). *A Framework for Understanding Poverty* (3rd Revised Edition). Highlands, TX: aha! Process.

Papolos, Demitri, & Papolos, Janice. (2002). *The Bipolar Child.* New York, NY: Broadway Books.

Tobias, Cynthia Ulrich. (1996). *Every Child Can Succeed.* Colorado Springs, CO: Focus on the Family Publishing.

Turecki, Stanley, with Tonner, Leslie. (2000). *The Difficult Child.* (2nd Revised Edition). New York, NY: Bantam Books.

Van den Bergh, B.R.H. (1990). The influence of maternal emotions during pregnancy on fetal and neonatal behavior. *Pre- & Peri-Natal Psychology Journal,* 5 (2), Winter, 119-130.

Vaughan, Christopher C. (1996). *How Life Begins: The Science of Life in the Womb.* New York, NY: Times Books.

By professional relationship

Matheson, Craig, D.O. Family physician (specializing in ADD/ADHD).Co-presenter with author Stressman on ADHD topics. Fremont, MI: Pine Medical Physicians Group.

Villet, Wanda, M.S.W. Attachment therapist. Created assessment tool for foster parents; author Stressman adapted it for this book. Blanchard, MI.

Weeks, Gailord, Ph.D. Clinical psychologist. Designed crisis intervention sequence in this book, which author Stressman adapted. Fremont, MI: Midwest Psychology.

By title

Children's Foster Care Manual. (2003). Family Independence Agency, State of Michigan. http://mfia.state.mi.us/olmweb/ex/cff/721.pdf.

Diagnostic and Statistical Manual of Mental Disorders (3rd Revised Edition). (1987). DSM-III-R. Washington, DC: American Psychiatric Association.

aha! Process, Inc.
P.O. Box 727
Highlands, TX 77562
(800) 424-9484
Fax: (281) 426-5600

www.ahaprocess.com

WANT YOUR OWN COPIES? WANT TO GIVE A COPY TO A FRIEND? PLEASE SEND:

_____ COPY/COPIES of *Parenting Someone Else's Child*

BOOKS: 1-4 books $22.00/each + $4.50 first book plus $2.00
                                  for each additional book, shipping/handling
           5 or more $15.00/each + 8% shipping/handling

MAIL TO:

NAME_____

ORGANIZATION _____

ADDRESS _____

_____

PHONE(S) _____

E-MAIL ADDRESS(ES) _____

_____

METHOD OF PAYMENT:

PURCHASE ORDER # _____

CREDIT CARD TYPE _____   EXP _____

CREDIT CARD # _____

CHECK $ _____   CHECK # _____

SUBTOTAL $ _____

SHIPPING $ _____

SALES TAX $ _____ 8.25% IN TEXAS

TOTAL $ _____